HISTORY OF CUBA;

OR,

Notes of a Traveller in the Tropics.

AMS PRESS
NEW YORK

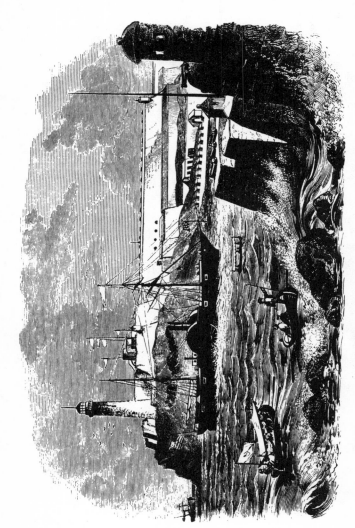

ENTRANCE TO THE HARBOR OF HAVANA.

HISTORY OF CUBA;

OR,

Notes of a Traveller in the Tropics.

BEING A

POLITICAL, HISTORICAL, AND STATISTICAL ACCOUNT OF THE
ISLAND, FROM ITS FIRST DISCOVERY TO THE
PRESENT TIME.

BY

MATURIN M. BALLOU.

L'ILE DE CUBA SEULE POURRAIT VALOIR UN ROYAUME.
L'Abbé Raynal.

ILLUSTRATED.

BOSTON:
PHILLIPS, SAMPSON AND COMPANY.
NEW YORK: J. C. DERBY.
PHILADELPHIA: LIPPINCOTT, GRAMBO & COMPANY.
1854.

Library of Congress Cataloging in Publication Data

Ballou, Maturin Murray, 1820-1895.
    History of Cuba.

    Reprint of the 1854 ed.
    1. Cuba--History. 2. Cuba--Description and travel.
I. Title.
F1763.B2 1972   917.291   70-161756
ISBN 0-404-00488-1

Reprinted from the edition of 1854, Boston, New York, and Philadelphia
First AMS edition published in 1972
Manufactured in the United States of America

International Standard Book Number: 0-404-00488-1

AMS PRESS INC.
NEW YORK, N. Y. 10003

T O

𝔚𝔦𝔰 𝔉𝔯𝔦𝔢𝔫𝔡,

FRANCIS A. DURIVAGE, ESQ.,

𝔄𝔰 𝔞 𝔰𝔪𝔞𝔩𝔩 𝔗𝔬𝔨𝔢𝔫 𝔬𝔣 ℜ𝔢𝔤𝔞𝔯𝔡 for

HIS EXCELLENCE IN THOSE QUALITIES WHICH CONSTITUTE STERLING MANHOOD ; AS A

TRUE AND WORTHY FRIEND ; AS A RIPE SCHOLAR, AND A GRACEFUL AUTHOR,

𝔗𝔥𝔦𝔰 𝔙𝔬𝔩𝔲𝔪𝔢

I S

CORDIALLY DEDICATED

B Y

THE AUTHOR.

PREFACE.

THE remarkable degree of interest expressed on all sides, at the present time, relative to the island of Cuba, has led the author of the following pages to place together in this form a series of notes from his journal, kept during a brief residence upon the island. To these he has prefixed a historical glance at the political story of Cuba, that may not be unworthy of preservation. The fact that the subject-matter was penned in the hurry of observation upon the spot, and that it is thus a simple record of what would be most likely to engage and interest a stranger, is his excuse for the desultory character of the work. So critically is the island now situated, in a political point of view, that ere this book shall have passed through an edition, it may be no longer a dependency of Spain, or may have become the theatre of scenes to which its former convulsions shall bear no parallel.

In preparing the volume for the press, the author has felt the want of books of reference, bearing a late date. Indeed, there are none ; and the only very modern records are those written in the desultory manner of hurried travellers. To the admirable work of the learned Ramon de la Sagra, — a monument of industry and intelligence, — the author of the following pages has been indebted for historical suggestions and data. For the privilege of consulting this, and other Spanish books and pamphlets, relative to the interests and history of the island, the author is indebted to the Hon. Edward Everett, who kindly placed them at his disposal. Where statistics were concerned, the several authorities have been carefully collated, and the most responsible given. The writer has preferred to offer the fresh memories of a pleasant trip to the tropics, to attempting a labored volume abounding in figures and statistics ; and trusts that this summer book of a summer clime may float lightly upon the sea of public favor.   M. M. B.

1*

CONTENTS.

CHAPTER I.

CHAPTER II.

CHAPTER III.

CHAPTER IV.

CHAPTER V.

CHAPTER VI.

CHAPTER VII.

CHAPTER VIII.

CHAPTER IX.

CHAPTER X.

CHAPTER XI.

CHAPTER XII.

CHAPTER XIII.

CHAPTER XIV.

CHAPTER XV.

CHAPTER XVI.

HISTORY OF CUBA.

CHAPTER I.

THE island of Cuba, one of the earliest discoveries of
the great admiral, has been known to Europe since 1492,
and has borne, successively, the names of Juana,* Fernandina, Santiago and Ave Maria, having found refuge at last
in the aboriginal appellation. Soon after its discovery by
Columbus, it was colonized by Spaniards from St. Domingo,
but was considered mainly in the light of a military depôt,
by the home government, in its famous operations at that

---

* In honor of Prince John, son of Ferdinand and Isabella. Changed to
Fernandina on the death of Ferdinand ; afterwards called Ave Maria,
in honor of the Holy Virgin. Cuba is the Indian name.

period in Mexico. The fact that it was destined to prove the richest jewel in the Castilian crown, and a mine of wealth to the Spanish treasury, was not dreamed of at this stage of its history. Even the enthusiastic followers of Cortez, who sought that fabulous El Dorado of the New World, had no golden promise to hold forth for this gem of the Caribbean Sea.

The Spanish colonists from St. Domingo found the island inhabited by a most peculiar native race, hospitable, inoffensive, timid, fond of the dance and the rude music of their own people, yet naturally indolent and lazy, from the character of the climate they inhabited. They had some definite idea of God and heaven; and were governed by patriarchs, or kings, whose word was law, and whose age gave them precedence. They had few weapons of offence or defence, and knew not the use of the bow and arrow. Of course, they were at once subjected by the new comers, who reduced them to a state of slavery; and, proving hard taskmasters, the poor, over-worked natives died in scores, until they had nearly disappeared, when the home government granted permission to import a cargo of negroes from the coast of Africa to labor upon the ground, and to seek for gold, which was thought to exist in the river-courses.*

---

* " Thus," exclaims the pious Arrati, " began that gathering of an infinite number of gentiles to the bosom of our holy religion, who would otherwise have perished in the darkness of paganism." Spain *has* liberal laws relative to the religious instruction of the slaves; but they are no better than a dead letter.

Thus early commenced the slave-trade of Cuba, a subject to which we shall have occasion more fully to refer.

Cuba became the head-quarters of the Spanish power in the west, forming the point of departure for those military expeditions which, though inconsiderable in numbers, were so formidable in the energy of the leaders, and in the arms, discipline, courage, ferocity, fanaticism and avarice, of their followers, that they were amply adequate to carry out the vast schemes of conquest for which they were designed. It was hence that Cortez marched to the conquest of Mexico, — a gigantic undertaking — one a slight glance at which will recall to the reader the period of history to which we would direct his attention. Landing upon the continent, with a little band, scarcely more than half the complement of a modern regiment, he prepared to traverse an unknown country, thronged by savage tribes, with whose character, habits and means of defence, he was wholly unacquainted. This romantic adventure, worthy of the palmiest days of chivalry, was crowned with success, though checkered with various fortune, and stained with bloody episodes, that prove how the threads of courage and ferocity are inseparably blended in the woof and warp of Spanish character. It must be remembered, however, that the spirit of the age was harsh, relentless and intolerant; and, that if the Aztecs, idolaters and sacrificers of human victims, found no mercy at the hands of the fierce Catholics whom Cortez

commanded, neither did the Indians of our own section of
the continent fare much better at the hands of men profess-
ing a purer faith, and coming to these shores, not as war-
riors, with the avowed purpose of conquest, but themselves
persecuted fugitives.

As the first words that greeted the ears of the Plymouth
colonists were "Welcome, Englishmen!" uttered by a poor
native, who had learned them from the fishermen off the
northern coast, so were the Spaniards at first kindly wel-
comed by the aborigines they encountered in the New
World. Yet, in the north-east and south-west the result
was the same: it mattered little whether the stranger was
Roman Catholic or Protestant; whether he came clad in
steel, or robed in the garments of peace; whether he spoke
the harsh English, the soft French, or the rich Castilian
tongue. The inexorable laws which govern races were rig-
idly enforced; the same drama was everywhere enacted, the
white race enjoying a speedy triumph. There were episod-
ical struggles, fierce and furious, but unavailing; here
Guatimozin, there Philip of Pokanoket — here a battle, there
a massacre.

The Spanish general encountered a people who had at-
tained a far higher point of art and civilization than their
red brethren of the north-east part of the continent. Vast
pyramids, imposing sculptures, curious arms, fanciful garments, various kinds of manufactures, the relics of which
still strangely interest the student of the past, filled the in-

vaders with surprise. There was much that was curious and startling in their mythology, and the capital of the Mexican empire presented a singular and fascinating spectacle to the eyes of Cortez. The rocky amphitheatre in the midst of which it was built still remains unchanged, but the vast lake which surrounded it, traversed by causeways, and covered with floating gardens, laden with flowers and perfume, is gone. The star of the Aztec dynasty set in blood. In vain did the inhabitants of the conquered city, roused to madness by the cruelty and extortion of the victors, expel them from their midst. Cortez refused to flee further than the shore; the light of his burning galleys rekindled the desperate valor of his followers, and Mexico fell, as a few years after did Peru under the perfidy and sword of Pizarro, thus completing the scheme of conquest, and giving Spain a colonial empire more splendid than that of any other power in Christendom.

Of the agents in this vast scheme of territorial aggrandizement, we see Cortez dying in obscurity, and Pizarro assassinated in his palace, while retributive justice has overtaken the monarchy at whose behests the richest portions of the western continent were violently wrested from their native possessors. If "the wild and warlike, the indolent and the semi-civilized, the bloody Aztec, the inoffensive Peruvian, the fierce Araucanian, all fared alike" at the hands of Spain, it must be confessed that their wrongs have been signally avenged. "The horrid atrocities practised at

2

home and abroad," says Edward Everett, "not only in the Netherlands, but in every city of the northern country, cried to Heaven for vengeance upon Spain; nor could she escape it. She intrenched herself behind the eternal Cordilleras; she took to herself the wings of the morning, and dwelt in the uttermost parts of the sea; but even there the arm of retribution laid hold of her, and the wrongs of both hemispheres were avenged by her degeneracy and fall."

So rapid a fall is almost without a parallel in the history of the world. Less than three centuries from the time when she stood without a rival in the extent and wealth of her colonial possessions, she beheld herself stripped, one by one, of the rich exotic jewels of her crown. Her vice-regal coronet was torn from her grasp. Mexico revolted; the South American provinces threw off her yoke; and now, though she still clutches with febrile grasp the brightest gem of her transatlantic possessions, the island of Cuba, yet it is evident that she cannot long retain its ownership. The "ever-faithful" island has exhibited unmistakable symptoms of infidelity, its demonstrations of loyalty being confined to the government officials and the hireling soldiery. The time will surely come when the last act of the great drama of historical retribution will be consummated, and when, in spite of the threatening batteries of the Moro and the Punta, and the bayonets of Spanish legions, *siempre fiel* will no longer be the motto of the Queen of the Antilles.

The history of Cuba is deficient in events of a stirring character, and yet not devoid of interest. Columbus found it inhabited, as we have already remarked, by a race whose manners and character assimilated with the mild climate of this terrestrial paradise. Although the Spanish conquerors have left us but few details respecting these aborigines, yet we know with certainty, from the narratives of the great discoverer and his followers, that they were docile and generous, but, at the same time, inclined to ease; that they were well-formed, grave, and far from possessing the vivacity of the natives of the south of Europe. They expressed themselves with a certain modesty and respect, and were hospitable to the last degree. Their labor was limited to the light work necessary to provide for the wants of life, while the bounteous climate of the tropics spared the necessity of clothing. They preferred hunting and fishing to agriculture; and beans and maize, with the fruits that nature gave them in abundance, rendered their diet at once simple and nutritious. They possessed no quadrupeds of any description, except a race of voiceless dogs, of whose existence we have no proof but the assertion of the discoverers.

The island was politically divided into nine provinces, namely, Baracoa, Bayaguitizi, Macaca, Bayamo, Camaguey, Jagua, Cueyba, Habana and Haniguanica. At the head of each was a governor, or king, of whose laws we have no record, or even tradition. An unbroken peace reigned among them, nor did they turn their hands against any other people. Their priests, called *Behiques*, were fanatics, superstitious to the last degree, and kept the people in fear by gross extravagances. They were not cannibals, nor did they employ human sacrifices, and are represented as distinguished by a readiness to receive the Gospel.

The capital of the island was Baracoa,* erected into a city and bishopric in 1518, but both were transferred to Santiago de Cuba in 1522. In the year 1538, the city of Havana was surprised by a French corsair and reduced to ashes. The French and English buccaneers of the West Indies, whose hatred the Spaniards early incurred, were for a long time their terror and their scourge. Enamored of the wild life they led, unshackled by any laws but the rude regulations they themselves adopted, unrefined by intercourse with the gentler sex, consumed by a thirst for adventure, and brave to ferocity, these fierce rovers, for many years, were the actual masters of the gulf. They feared no enemy, and spared none; their vessels, constantly on the watch for booty, were ever ready, on the appearance of a galleon, to swoop down like an eagle on its prey. The romance of the sea owes some of its most thrilling chapters to the fearful exploits of these buccaneers. Their *coup de main* on Havana attracted the attention of De Soto, the governor of the island, to the position and advantages of the

---

* Here Leo X. erected the first cathedral in Cuba. Baracoa is situated on the north coast, at the eastern extremity of the island, and contains some three thousand inhabitants, mixed population.

port at which the Spanish vessels bound for the peninsula with the riches of New Mexico were accustomed to touch, and he accordingly commenced to fortify it. It increased in population by degrees, and became the habitual gubernatorial residence, until the home government made it the capital of the island in 1589, on the appointment of the first Captain-general, Juan de Tejada.

The native population soon dwindled away under the severe sway of the Spaniards, who imposed upon them tasks repugnant to their habits, and too great for their strength.

Velasquez, one of the earliest governors of the island, appears to have been an energetic and efficient magistrate, and to have administered affairs with vigor and intelligence ; but his harsh treatment of the aborigines will ever remain a stain upon his memory. A native chief, whose only crime was that of taking up arms in defence of the integrity of his little territory, fell into the hands of Velasquez, and was burned alive, as a punishment for his patriotism.* It is no wonder that under such treatment the native population disappeared so rapidly that the Spaniards were forced to supply their places by laborers of hardier character.

We have seen that the office of captain-general was established in 1589, and, with a succession of incumbents, the

---

* The words of this unfortunate chief (Hatuey), extorted by the torments he suffered, were, " *Prefiero el infierno al cielo si en cielo ha Españoles.*" (I prefer hell to heaven, if there are Spaniards in heaven.)

office has been maintained until the present day, retaining the same functions and the same extraordinary powers. The object of the Spanish government is, and ever has been, to derive as much revenue as possible from the island; and the exactions imposed upon the inhabitants have increased in proportion as other colonies of Spain, in the western world, have revolted and obtained their independence. The imposition of heavier burthens than those imposed upon any other people in the world has been the reward of the proverbial loyalty of the Cubans; while the epithet of " ever-faithful," bestowed by the crown, has been their only recompense for their steady devotion to the throne. But for many years this lauded loyalty has existed only in appearance, while discontent has been fermenting deeply beneath the surface.

The Cubans owe all the blessings they enjoy to Providence alone (so to speak), while the evils which they suffer are directly referable to the oppression of the home government. Nothing short of a military despotism could maintain the connection of such an island with a mother country more than three thousand miles distant; and accordingly we find the captain-general of Cuba invested with unlimited power. He is, in fact, a viceroy appointed by the crown of Spain, and accountable only to the reigning sovereign for his administration of the colony. His rule is absolute; he has the power of life and death and liberty in his hands. He can, by his arbitrary will, send into exile any person whatever, be his name or rank what it may, whose residence in the island he considers prejudicial to the royal interest, even if he has committed no overt act. He can suspend the operation of the laws and ordinances, if he sees fit to do so ; can destroy or confiscate property ; and, in short, the island may be said to be perpetually in a state of siege.

Such is the infirmity of human nature that few individuals can be trusted with despotic power without abusing it; and accordingly we find very few captain-generals whose administration will bear the test of rigid examination. Few men who have governed Cuba have consulted the true interests of the Creoles; in fact, they are not appointed for that purpose, but merely to look after the crown revenue. An office of such magnitude is, of course, a brilliant prize, for which the grandees of Spain are constantly struggling; and the means by which an aspirant is most likely to secure the appointment presupposes a character of an inferior order. The captain-general knows that he cannot reckon on a long term of office, and hence he takes no pains to study the interests or gain the good-will of the Cubans. He has a two-fold object in view,— to keep the revenue well up to the mark, and to enrich himself as speedily as possible. Hence, the solemn obligations entered into by Spain with the other powers for the suppression of the African slave-trade are a dead letter ; for, with very few exceptions, the captains-general of Cuba have connived at the illegal importation of slaves, receiving for their complaisance a large percentage on the value of each one landed on the island; for, though the slavers do not discharge their living freights at the more frequented ports, still their arrival is a matter of public notoriety, and it is impossible that, with the present system of espionage, the authorities can be ignorant of such an event. Nor can we imagine that the home government is less well-informed upon the subject, though they assume a politic ignorance of the violation of the law. Believing that the importation of slaves is essential to the maintenance of the present high revenue, Spain illustrates the rule that there are none so blind as those who do not wish to see. It is only the cheapness of labor, resulting from the importation of slaves, that enables the planters to pour into the government treasury from twenty to twenty-four millions of dollars annually. Of this we may speak more fully hereafter.

In 1760, the invasion and conquest of the island by the British forms one of the most remarkable epochs in its history. This event excited the fears of Spain, and directed the attention of the government to its importance in a political point of view. On its restoration, at the treaty of peace concluded between the two governments in the following year, Spain seriously commenced the work of fortifying the Havana, and defending and garrisoning the island generally.

The elements of prosperity contained within the limits of this peerless island required only a patriotic and enlightened administration for their development; and the germ of its civilization was stimulated by the appointment of General Don Luis de las Casas to the post of captain-general. During the administration of this celebrated man, whose memory is cherished with fond respect by the Cubans, The Patriotic Society of Havana was formed, with the noble idea of diffusing education throughout the island, and introducing a taste for classical literature, through his instrumentality, while the press was also established in the capital, by the publication of the *Papel Periodico.*

In the first third of the present century, the *intendente,* Don Alejandro Ramirez, labored to regulate the revenues and economical condition of the country, and called the attention of the government to the improvement of the white population. But the most important concession obtained of the metropolitan government, the freedom of commerce, was due to the patriotic exertions of Don Francisco de Arranjo, the most illustrious name in Cuban annals, "one," says the Countess Merlin, "who may be quoted as a model of the humane and peaceful virtues," and "who was," says Las Casas, "a jewel of priceless value to the glory of the nation, a protector for Cuba, and an accomplished statesman for the monarchy." Even the briefest historical sketch (and this record pretends to no more) would be incomplete without particular mention of this excellent man.

He was born at Havana, May 22d, 1765. Left an orphan at a very early age, he managed the family estate, while a mere boy, with a discretion and judgment which

would have done honor to a man of mature age.   **Turning**
his attention to the study of the law, he was admitted to
practice in the mother country, where for a considerable
period he acted as the agent for the municipality of Havana,
and, being thoroughly acquainted with the capabilities of the
island, and the condition and wants of his countrymen, he
succeeded in procuring the amelioration of some of the most
flagrant abuses of the colonial system.   By his exertions, the
staple productions of the island were so much increased that
the revenue, in place of falling short of the expenses of the
government, as his enemies had predicted, soon yielded a large
surplus.   He early raised his voice against the iniquitous
slave-trade, and suggested the introduction of white laborers,
though he perceived that the abolition of slavery was im-
practicable.   It was owing to his exertions that the duty on
coffee, spirits and cotton, was remitted for a period of ten
years, and that machinery was allowed to be imported free
of duty to the island.

The *Junta de Fomento* (society for improvement) and
the Chamber of Commerce were the fruits of his indefatigable efforts.   Of the latter institution he was for a long time
the Syndic, refusing to receive the perquisites attached to
the office, as he did the salaries of the same and other offices
that he filled during his useful life.   While secretary of the
Chamber, he distinguished himself by his bold opposition to
the schemes of the infamous Godoy (the Prince of Peace),
the minion of the Queen of Spain, who, claiming to be pro-

tector of the Chamber of Commerce, demanded the receipts of the custom-house at Havana. He not only defeated the plans of Godoy, but procured the relinquishment of the royal monopoly of tobacco. His patriotic services were appreciated by the court at Madrid, although at times he was the inflexible opponent of its schemes. The cross of the order of Charles III. showed the esteem in which he was held by that monarch. Yet, with a modesty which did him honor, he declined to accept a title of nobility which was afterwards offered to him. In 1813, when, by the adoption of the constitution of 1812, Cuba became entitled to representation in the general Cortes, he visited Madrid as a deputy, and there achieved the crowning glory of his useful life,— the opening of the ports of Cuba to foreign trade. In 1817 he returned to his native island with the rank of Counsellor of State, Financial Intendente of Cuba, and wearing the grand cross of the order of Isabella. He died in 1837, at the age of seventy-two, after a long and eminently useful life, bequeathing large sums for various public purposes and charitable objects in the island. Such a man is an honor to any age or nation, and the Cubans do well to cherish his memory, which, indeed, they seem resolved, by frequent and kindly mention, to keep ever green.

Fostered by such men, the resources of Cuba, both physical and intellectual, received an ample and rapid development. The youth of the island profited by the means of instruction now liberally placed at their disposal: the sciences and belles-lettres were assiduously cultivated; agriculture and internal industry were materially improved, and an ambitious spirit evoked, which subsequent periods of tyranny and misrule have not been able, with all their baneful influences, entirely to erase.

The visitor from abroad is sure to hear the people refer to this " golden period," as they call it, of their history, the influence of which, so far from passing away, appears to grow and daily increase with them. It raised in their bosoms one spirit and trust which they sadly needed,— that of self-reliance,— and showed them of what they were capable, under liberal laws and judicious government.

VIEW OF THE IMPERIAL DEL PASEO.

CHAPTER II.

The constitution of 1812 — Revolution of La Granja — Political aspect of the island — Discontent among the Cubans — The example before them — Simon Bolivar, the Liberator — Revolutions of 1823 and 1826 — General Lorenzo and the constitution — The assumption of extraordinary power by Tacon — Civil war threatened — Tacon sustained by royal authority — Despair of the Cubans — Military rule — A foreign press established — Programme of the liberal party — General O'Donnell — The spoils — Influence of the climate.

WHEN the French invasion of Spain in 1808 produced the constitution of 1812, Cuba was considered entitled to enjoy its benefits, and the year 1820 taught the Cubans the advantage to be derived by a people from institutions based on the principle of popular intervention in public affairs. The condition of the nation on the death of Ferdinand VII. obliged Queen Christina to rely on the liberal party for a triumph over the pretensions of the Infante Don Carlos to the crown, and to assure the throne of Donna Isabella II., and the *Estatuto Real* (royal statute) was proclaimed in Spain and Cuba. The Cubans looked forward, as in 1812 and 1820, to a representation in the national congress, and the enjoyment of the same liberty conceded to the Peninsula. An institution was then established in Havana,

3

with branches in the island, called the Royal Society for Improvement, already alluded to in our brief notice of Don Francisco Arranjo. The object of this society was to aid and protect the progress of agriculture and commerce; and it achieved a vast amount of good. At the same time, the press, within the narrow limits conceded to it, discussed with intelligence and zeal the interests of the country, and diffused a knowledge of them.

In 1836 the revolution known as that of La Granja, provoked and sustained by the progressionists against the moderate party, destroyed the "Royal Statute," and proclaimed the old constitution of 1812. The queen-mother, then Regent of Spain, convoked the constituent Cortes, and summoned deputies from Cuba.

Up to this time, various political events, occurring within a brief period, had disturbed but slightly and accidentally the tranquillity of this rich province of Spain. The Cubans, although sensible of the progress of public intelligence and wealth, under the protection of a few enlightened governors, and through the influence of distinguished and patriotic individuals, were aware that these advances were slow, partial and limited, that there was no regular system, and that the public interests, confided to officials intrusted with unlimited power, and liable to the abuses inseparable from absolutism, frequently languished, or were betrayed by a cupidity which impelled despotic authorities to enrich themselves in every possible way at the expense of popular suffering.   Added to these sources of discontent was the powerful influence exerted over the intelligent portion of the people by the portentous spectacle of the rapidly-increasing greatness of the United States, where a portion of the Cuban youths were wont to receive their education, and to learn the value of a national independence based on democratic principles, principles which they were apt freely to discuss after returning to the island.

There also were the examples of Mexico and Spanish South America, which had recently conquered with their blood their glorious emancipation from monarchy.   Liberal ideas were largely diffused by Cubans who had travelled in Europe, and there imbibed the spirit of modern civilization. But, with a fatuity and obstinacy which has always characterized her, the mother country resolved to ignore these causes of discontent, and, instead of yielding to the popular current, and introducing a liberal and mild system of government, drew the reins yet tighter, and even curtailed many of the privileges formerly accorded to the Cubans. It is a blind persistence in the fated principle of despotic domination which has relaxed the moral and political bonds uniting the two countries, instilled gall into the hearts of the governed, and substituted the dangerous obedience of terror for the secure loyalty of love.   This severity of the home government has given rise to several attempts to throw off the Spanish yoke.

The first occurred in 1823, when the Liberator, Simon

Bolivar, offered to aid the disaffected party by throwing an
invading force into the island. The conspiracy then formed,
by the aid of the proffered expedition, for which men were
regularly enlisted and enrolled, would undoubtedly have
ended in the triumph of the insurrection, had it not been
discovered and suppressed prematurely, and had not the
governments of the United States, Great Britain and
France, intervened in favor of Spain. In 1826 some Cuban emigrants, residing in Caraccas, attempted a new expedition, which failed, and caused the imprisonment and execution of two patriotic young men, Don Francisco de Agüero,
y Velazco, and Don Bernabé Sanchez, sent to raise the department of the interior. In 1828 there was a yet more
formidable conspiracy, known as *El Aguila Negra* (the
black eagle). The efforts of the patriots proved unavailing, foiled by the preparation and power of the government,
which seems to be apprised by spies of every intended
movement for the cause of liberty in Cuba.

We have alluded to the revolution of La Granja, in
Spain, and we have now briefly to consider its effects on the
island of Cuba, then under the sway of General Don Miguel Tacon. We shall have occasion to refer more than
once, in the course of our records of the island, to the administration of Tacon; for he made his mark upon Cuba,
and, though he governed it with an iron hand and a stern
will, as we shall see, yet he did much to improve its physical condition, even as Louis Napoleon, despot though he be,

has already vastly beautified and improved the sanitary condition of the city of Paris.

The first place on the island which received intelligence of the revolution of La Granja, and the oath to the constitution of 1812 by the Queen-Regent of Spain, was Santiago de Cuba, the capital of the eastern department. It was then commanded by General Lorenzo, who immediately assembled the authorities, corporations and functionaries, in pursuance of the example of his predecessors,—who, without waiting for the orders of the higher authority of the island, had, under similar circumstances, prepared to obey the supreme government of the nation,— and proclaimed through his department the Code of Cadiz, without any opposition, and to the general joy of Spaniards and Cubans. His first acts were to reëstablish the constitutional *ayuntamiento*, the national militia, the liberty of the press, and all other institutions, on the same footing as in 1823, when King Ferdinand recovered absolute authority, and made arrangements for the election of deputies to the new Cortes.

Tacon, who was not a friend to liberal institutions, and who was fixed in his idea that the new constitution would convulse the country, notwithstanding his knowledge of the state of things when this law was actually in force in Cuba, was quite indignant when he heard what had transpired. Knowing that he could not compel General Lorenzo to abrogate the constitution he had proclaimed, he forthwith cut off all communication with the eastern department, and

3*

formed a column to invade it, and to restore the old order of things by force. This was a bold, impolitic and dangerous move, because this resolve was contrary to the wishes of the supreme government and public opinion, which would not fail to see treason in the act of Gen. Tacon, against the mother country.

Although the royal proclamation which announced to Tacon the establishment of the constitution in Spain intimated forthcoming orders for the election of deputies in Cuba to the general Cortes, still he considered that his commission as captain-general authorized him, under the circumstances, to carry out his own will, and suppress at once the movement set on foot by General Lorenzo, on the ground of its danger to the peace of the island, and the interests of Spain. The royal order, which opened the way for his attacks upon the Cuban people, after a confused preamble, confers on the captain-general all the authority appertaining in time of war to a Spanish governor of a city in a state of siege, authorizing him in any circumstances and by his proper will to suspend any public functionary, whatever his rank, civil, military, or ecclesiastical ; to banish any resident of the island, without preferring any accusations ; to modify any law, or suspend its operations ;*

* " En su consecuencia da S. M. á V. E. la mas ámplia é ilimitada autorizacion, no tan solo para separar de esa Isla á las personas empleadas ó no empleadas, cualquiera que sea su destino, rango, clase ó condicion, cuya permanencia en ella crea prejudicial, ó que le infunda recelos su conducta pública ó privada, reemplazandolas interinamente con servidores fieles á S. M. y que merezcan á V. E. toda su confianza, sino tambien para suspender la ejecucion de cualesquiera órdenes ó providencias generales

disobey with impunity any regulation emanating from the Spanish government; to dispose of the public revenues at his will; and, finally, to act according to his pleasure, winding up with recommending a moderate use of the confidence evinced by the sovereign in according power so ample.

Although the captains-general of Cuba have always been invested with extraordinary power, we believe that these items of unlimited authority were first conferred upon Vivez in 1825, when the island was menaced by an invasion of the united forces of Mexico and Columbia. In these circumstances, and emanating from an absolute authority, like that of Ferdinand VII., a delegation of power which placed the destinies of the island at the mercy of its chief ruler might have had the color of necessity; but to continue such a delegation of authority in time of peace is a most glaring and inexcusable blunder.

Meanwhile Tacon assembled a column of picked companies of the line, the provincial military and rural cavalry, and placed them, under the orders of General Gascue, in the town of Guines, hoping by this great parade and preparation to impose on General Lorenzo, and strike terror into the inhabitants of the whole island. He also adroitly worked by secret agents upon the forces at Santiago de Cuba, and thus by cunning and adroitness brought about quite a reäction in the public sentiment.

espedidas sobre todos los ramos de la administracion en aquella parte en que V. E. considere conveniente al real servicio, debiendo ser en todo caso provisionales estas medidas, y dar V. E. cuenta á S. M. para su soberana aprobacion."—*From the Royal Ordinance conferring unlimited powers on the Captains-general of Cuba.*

Under these circumstances, if General Lorenzo, master of the eastern department, with two regiments of regular troops, all the national militia, all devoted to the new order of things and ready to obey his will, had marched upon Puerto Principe, the capital of the centre, where the garrison was not strong enough to oppose him, and had there proclaimed the constitutional code through the authority of the royal *Audiencia*, Gen. Tacon would unquestionably have desisted from his opposition, and relinquished the command of the island. Cuba would then have enjoyed the same political rights as the rest of Spain, and have escaped the horrors of tyranny which have since weighed her down. But Gen. Lorenzo proved weak, let slip the golden opportunity of triumphing over Tacon, and returned to Spain in the vain hope that the supreme government would sustain him. In the mean time, Tacon sent his body of soldiery to Santiago, their arrival being signalized by the establishment of a military commission to try and punish all who had been engaged innocently in establishing the fallen constitution. The commandant Moya presided, and the advocate Miret was held as counsel.

No sooner had this barbarous tribunal commenced its proceedings, than no Creole belonging to families of influence could look upon himself as safe from persecution, since nearly all of them had hastened to obey the orders of General Lorenzo, and, like him, taken oath to the constitution. Many men of rank, reputation and education, including several respectable clergymen, fell under the ban of the military commission. Some were thrown into the prisons of Santiago de Cuba, some banished for a given period, and many emigrated to avoid the horrors of a Spanish dungeon, and the greater part in one way or another were torn from the bosoms of their families. Of the soldiers who faith-fully obeyed their officers, about five hundred were con-demned to work in the streets of Havana, with their feet shackled. Such are the measures meted out by despotism to those who have the misfortune to live under its iron yoke.

Tacon triumphed, yet the Cubans did not utterly despair. They cherished the hope that the Spanish government would recognize the legality of their proceedings in the eastern department; but they were doomed to disappoint-ment. The Cuban deputies presented themselves in the Spanish capital, and offered their credentials. But they were referred to a committee of men profoundly ignorant of the feelings, opinions and condition, of the Cuban people, or deriving what few notions they possessed from those inter-ested on the side of Tacon. The deputies were not allowed a seat in the Cortes, and the government decided that the provisions of the constitution should not apply to Cuba, but that it should be governed by special laws. Since then, the island has been ruled by the arbitrary will of the cap-tains-general, without intervention of the Spanish Cortes, without the intervention of the island, and, what is almost inconceivable, at first thought, without the direct action even of the sovereign authority.

Tacon, now that the royal authority had sustained his action, was more despotic than ever. It is true that he introduced some legal and municipal reforms; that he embellished the capital, and improved its health; but under him the censorship of the press was almost prohibitory. The local *ayuntamientos*, which, at the most despotic epoch, had frequently produced happy effects, by representing to the sovereign the wants of the country, were shorn of their privileges, and their attributes confined to the collection and distribution of the municipal funds. Tacon is also charged with promoting the jealousies naturally existing between Spaniards and Creoles, and with completely subjecting the civil courts to military tribunals.

" In a state of agitation in the public mind, and disorder in the government," says the author of an able pamphlet entitled " *Cuba y su Gobierno*," to whom we are indebted for invaluable information that could only be imparted by a Creole, " with the political passions of Spaniards and Cubans excited; the island reduced from an integral part of the monarchy to the condition of a colony, and with no other political code than the royal order, conferring unlimited power upon the chief authority; the country bowed down under the weighty tyranny of two military commissions established in the capitals of the eastern and western departments; with the prisons filled with distinguished patriots; deprived of representation in the Cortes; the *ayuntamientos* prohibited the right of petition; the press forbidden to enunciate the state of public opinion, closed the administration of General Don Miguel Tacon in the island of Cuba, the most calamitous, beyond a question, that this country has suffered since its discovery by the Spaniards."

The liberal party of Cuba, denied the expression of their views in the local prints, and anxious to present their wants and their grievances before the home government, conceived the ingenious idea of establishing organs abroad. Two papers were accordingly published; one at Paris, called "*El Correo de Ultramar*," and one at Madrid, entitled "*El Observador*," edited by distinguished Cubans.* It is scarcely necessary to say that these produced no favorable result, and the people of the island became convinced that the mother country was resolved to persevere in the plan of ruling Cuba with a rod of iron, indifferent alike to her tears and her remonstrances.

The programme of the liberal party was exceedingly moderate, petitioning only for the following concessions: 1st, That a special ministry, devoted to Cuban affairs, should be established at Madrid; 2d, That a legal organ of communication between Spain and Cuba should be established in the island, to represent the well-defined interests of the metropolis and the colony; 3d, That some latitude should be given to the press, now controlled by a triple censorship;

---

* " La Verdad," a paper devoted to Cuban interests, established in New York in 1848, and conducted with signal ability, is distributed gratuitously, the expense being defrayed by contributions of Cubans and the friends of Cuban independence. This is the organ of the annexation party, organized by exiles in this country.

4th, That efficacious means should be adopted for the complete suppression of the barbarous traffic in African slaves; 5th, That the government should permit the establishment of societies for the improvement of the white inhabitants; 6th, That the island should be relieved of the enormous weight of the contributions now levied upon her. None of these privileges, however, have been conceded to suffering Cuba by the home government.

The first successor of General Tacon ruled Cuba with a spirit of moderation and temperance, seeking to conciliate the liberals, and giving hopes of great reforms, which as yet have never been accomplished. During the administration of the Prince de Aglona, a superior tribunal, the Royal Pretorial Audience, was established in Havana, to take cognizance of civil suits in cases of appeal, and to resolve the doubts which the confused system of legislation produces at every step in the inferior tribunals. Gen. Valdes was the first and only official who granted free papers to the emancipated negroes who had served out their term of apprenticeship, and who opposed the African trade. He showed, by his example, that this infamous traffic may be destroyed in the country without a necessary resort to violent measures, but by the will of the captain-general.

General O'Donnell, as captain-general,* instead of re-

* General Leopold O'Donnell was appointed governor-general in 1843, continuing a little over four years to fill the lucrative position. His wife was a singular and most avaricious woman, engaged in many speculations upon the island, and shamefully abusing her husband's official influence for the purposes of pecuniary emolument.

pressing, encouraged the slave-trade, and a greater number of the unfortunate victims of human avarice were introduced into the island, during his administration, than during any like term since the conclusion of the treaty of 1817. Of course he vacated his post vastly enriched by the spoils, having doubtless received, as was declared, from one to two doubloons per head on every slave landed upon the island during his administration ; a sum that would alone amount to a fortune.

Of events which transpired during the administration of Roncali and Concha we may have occasion to speak hereafter, but with this more modern chapter in the history of the island the general reader is already conversant. It appears almost incredible that an intelligent people, within so short a distance of our southern coast, constantly visited by the citizens of a free republic, and having the example of successful revolt set them, by the men of the same race, both in the north and south, weighed down by oppressions almost without parallel, should never have aimed an effectual blow at their oppressors. It would seem that the softness of the unrivalled climate of those skies beneath which it is luxury only to exist has unnerved them, and that the effeminate spirit of the original inhabitants has descended in retribution to the posterity of the *conquistadores*.

4

CHAPTER III.

WE have noticed in the preceding chapter, the anomaly
of the political condition of Cuba, increasing in prosperity
and civilization, imbibing liberal ideas from its geographical
position, and yet denied participation in the few shadowy
rights which the peninsular subjects of the enfeebled, dis-
tracted and despotic parent monarchy enjoyed. We have
seen that, in later years, the adoption of more liberal ideas
by Spain produced no amelioration of the condition of the
colony; and that, on the other hand, a conformity to the
legal enactments of the mother country was punished as
treason. The result of the movement in the western department, under Tacon, showed the Cubans that they had
nothing to hope from Spain, while the cruelties of General
O'Donnell increased the great discontent and despair of the

people. They now became satisfied that the hope of legal reform was but a chimera; and a portion of the liberal party, seeing no issue from their insufferable position but that of revolution, boldly advocated the intervention of arms.

In 1848 a conspiracy was formed, in Cienfuegos and Trinidad, with the purpose of throwing off the Spanish yoke; but it was soon discovered, and crushed by the imprisonment of various individuals in the central department. The principal leader in this movement was General Narciso Lopez, who succeeded in effecting his escape to the United States, where he immediately placed himself in communication with several influential and liberal Creoles, voluntary and involuntary exiles, and established a correspondence with the remnant of the liberal party yet at liberty on the island, at the same time being aided in his plans by American sympathy. The result of the deliberations of himself, his correspondents and associates, was to try by the chances of war for the liberation of Cuba. The disastrous result of the expedition boldly undertaken for this purpose is already well known.

Before sketching the principal features of this attempt, we may be permitted to declare that, although we deplore the fate of those of our countrymen who perished in the adventure, though we readily concede that many of them were actuated by lofty motives, still we must condemn their action, and approve of the vigorous measures adopted by the federal government to suppress that species of reckless

adventure in which the *flibustiers* engaged. No amount
of sympathy with the sufferings of an oppressed people, no
combination of circumstances, no possible results, can excuse
the fitting out of a warlike expedition in the ports of a nation against the possessions of a friendly power. The flag
which has waved unstained in peace and war over a free
land for more than three quarters of a century, must remain
spotless to the last. The hopes of every free heart in the
world are centred on our banner, and we must see to it
that no speck dims the dazzling lustre of its stars. No
degree of pride at the daring gallantry displayed by the
little handful of invaders of Cuba, — a gallantry inherited
from a brave ancestry who displayed their valor in the holiest
of causes,— must blind our eyes to the character of the adventure which called it forth. We have tears for the fallen,
as brothers and men ; but our conscience must condemn their
errors. While, individually, we should rejoice to see Cuba
free, and an integral portion of the Union, nothing will ever
induce us to adopt the atrocious doctrine that the ends jus-
tify the means. But let us pass to a consideration of the
recent events in the records of the island.

Many of the leading patriots of the island undoubtedly
believed that the government of the United States would
second their efforts, if they should decide to unite themselves
to our republic, and boldly raise the banner of annexation.
A portion of the Cuban liberals adopted the motto, " Legal
Reform or Independence ; " and these two factions of the

patriots did not henceforth act in perfect concert with each
other — a most fatal error to the interests of both. Time
and circumstances favored the war and annexation party;
the people were more than ever discontented with a government which so oppressed them by a military despotism, and
by the enormous weight of the unjust taxation levied upon
them. We may here remark that the increase of the public
revenue, in the midst of so many elements of destruction
and ruin, can only be explained by the facility with which
the captain-general and royal stewards of the island invent
and arrange taxes, at their pleasure, and without a shadow
of propriety, or even precedent.

The *consuming* population of Cuba amounts to about
eight hundred thousand souls, and the total amount of taxes
and contributions of various forms is more than twenty-three
millions of dollars, in specie, per annum! It is hardly con-
ceivable that such a sum can be extorted from a population
whose wealth is precarious, and whose living is so costly.
With this revenue the government pays and supports an
army of over twenty thousand Peninsular troops in the
island; a vast number of employés, part of the clergy and
half the entire navy of Spain; the diplomatic corps in the
United States and Mexico; many officials of rank at home
in Spain; and the surplus is remitted to Spain, and spent
on the Peninsula on matters entirely foreign to the interests
of the island itself. A precious state of affairs!

The colored population of the island, both slaves and

4*

free, hated the Spaniards, for good reasons. The war party, moreover, reckoned on the genius of a leader (Lopez) trained to arms,* equal in talents to any of the Spanish generals, and beloved by the Spanish troops, as well as by the Cuban population; and they relied, also, as we have said, on the sympathy and ultimate aid of the United States government. It is undoubtedly true that interested parties in this country, prompted by mercenary motives, increased this latter delusion by false reports; while the Cuban conspirators, in turn, buoyed up the hopes of their friends in the United States, by glowing accounts of the patriotic spirit of the Creoles, and the extent of the preparations they were making for a successful revolt. General Lopez was actively arranging the means for an invasion, when, in 1849, the United States government threw terror into the ranks of the *flibustiers*, by announcing its determination to enforce the sacredness of treaty stipulations. This, for a time, frustrated the intended invasion.

In 1850 Lopez succeeded in effecting his first descent upon the island. Having succeeded in baffling the vigilance of the United States government, an expedition, consisting of six hundred and fifty-two men, was embarked on board two sailing-vessels and the steamer Creole, which conveyed the general and his staff. In the beginning of July the sailing-vessels left New Orleans, with orders to anchor

---

* His reputation as a cavalry officer was very distinguished, and he was commonly recognized as *La primera Lanza de España* (the first lance of Spain). — *Louis Schlesinger's Narrative of the Expedition.*

at Contoy, one of the Mugeres Islands, on the coast of Yucatan; the general followed, on the Creole, on the 7th. At the time when the troops were embarked on the Creole at Contoy, fifty-two of the number, who had been deceived as to the nature of the expedition, refused to follow the general, and were left on the island, with the intention of returning to the United States in the two schooners. General Lopez, after gaining some information from a fisherman he encountered, resolved to land at Cardenas, on the northern coast of the island, a hundred and twenty miles east of Havana. He calculated that he could surprise and master the garrison before the captain-general could possibly obtain intelligence of his departure from New Orleans. His plan was, to master the town, secure the authorities, intimidate the Spaniards, and then, sustained by the moral influence of victory, proceed to Matanzas by railroad.

Roncali, the captain-general, having received intelligence of the landing at Contoy, despatched several ships-of-war in that direction, to seize upon the general and his followers. The latter, however, escaped the snare, and effected his landing on the 19th. The garrison rushed to arms, and, while a portion of the troops, after immaterial loss, retired in good order to the suburbs, another, under the command of Governor Ceruti, intrenched themselves in the government-house, and gave battle to the invaders. After a sharp skirmish, the building being set on fire, they surrendered; the governor and two or three officers were made

prisoners, and the soldiers consented to join the revolutionary colors! Meanwhile, a body of one hundred invaders
seized upon the railroad station. The engines were fired
up, and the trains made ready to transport the invading
column to Matanzas.

But now came a pause. General Lopez, seeing that the
native population did not respond to his appeal, knew that
as soon as the news of the taking of Cardenas should be
circulated, he would be in a very critical situation. In
fact, the governor of Matanzas was soon on the march, at
the head of five hundred men. General Armero sailed from
Havana in the Pizarro, with a thousand infantry, while two
thousand five hundred picked troops, under the command of
General Count de Mirasol, were sent from Havana by the
railroad. Lopez saw that it would be madness to wait the
attack of these formidable columns, unsupported save by his
own immediate followers, and accordingly issued his orders
for the reëmbarkation of his band, yet without relinquish-
ing the idea of landing on some more favorable point of the
island.

That portion of the garrison which, in the beginning of
the affair, had retreated to the suburbs, finding itself reïn-
forced by a detachment of cavalry, attempted to cut off the
retreat of the invading general; but the deadly fire of the
latter's reserve decimated the horse, and the infantry, dis-
mayed at their destruction, took to rapid flight. The Creole
accordingly left the port without molestation, and before

the arrival of the government steam-frigate Pizarro. The
Spanish prisoners were landed at Cayo de Piedras, and
then Lopez, discovering the Pizarro in the distance, made
for the American continent, where the steamer was abandoned. General Lopez was arrested by the authorities of
Savannah, but liberated again, in deference to the public
clamor. The Creole was seized, confiscated and sold. The
invaders disbanded; and thus this enterprise terminated.

A less enterprising and determined spirit than that of
General Lopez would have been completely broken by the
failure of his first attempts, the inactivity of the Cubans,
the hostility of the American government, and the formidable forces and preparations of the Spanish officials. He
believed, however, that the Cubans were ripe for revolt;
that public opinion in the United States would nullify the
action of the federal government; and that, if he could once
gain a foothold in the island, the Spanish troops would
desert in such numbers to his banners that the preponderance of power would soon be upon his side; and, with these
views, he once more busied himself, with unremitting industry, to form another expedition.

Meanwhile, the daring attack upon Cardenas, while it
demonstrated the determination of the invading party,
caused great anxiety in the mind of General Roncali.
True, he had at his disposal an army of more than twenty
thousand regular troops; but he was by no means sure of
their loyalty, and he therefore determined to raise a local

militia ; but, as he suffered only Spaniards to enlist in it,
he aroused the jealousy of the Cuban-born inhabitants, and
thus swelled the force of opposition against the government.
General Lopez was informed of this fact, and based new
hopes upon the circumstance.

The Spanish government, having recalled Roncali, appointed Don José de la Concha captain-general of the
island, and the severity of his sway reminded the inhabitants
of the iron rule of Tacon.   It was during his administration
that Lopez effected his second landing at Playitas, sixty
miles west of Havana.   Several partial insurrections, which
had preceded this event, easily suppressed, as it appears, by
the Spanish government, but exaggerated in the accounts
despatched to the friends of Cuba in the United States,
inflamed the zeal of Lopez, and made him believe that the
time for a successful invasion had at length arrived.*   He
was so confident, at one time, of the determination and
ability of the Cubans alone to secure their independence,
that he wished to embark without any force, and throw himself among them.   It was this confidence that led him to
embark with only four hundred ill-armed men on board the
little steamer Pampero, on the 2d of August, 1851.   This

* "The general showed me much of his correspondence from the island.
It represented a pervading anxiety for his arrival, on the part of the Creole
population.   His presence alone, to head the insurrection, which would
then become general, was all they called for ; his presence and a supply
of arms, of which they were totally destitute.   The risings already made
were highly colored in some of the communications addressed to him from
sources of unquestionable sincerity."—*Louis Schlesinger's Narrative of
the Expedition.*

force consisted mostly of Americans, but embraced forty-nine Cubans in its ranks, with several German and Hungarian officers; among the latter, General Pragay, one of the heroes of the Hungarian revolution, who was second in command to General Lopez on this occasion.

Many of the foreign officers spoke little, if any, English, and mutual jealousies and insubordinations soon manifested themselves in the little band. They were composed of fierce spirits, and had come together without any previous drilling or knowledge of each other. It was not the intention of the commander-in-chief to sail direct for Cuba, but to go to the neighborhood of St. John's river, Florida, and get a supply of artillery, ammunition, extra arms, etc. He then proposed to land somewhere in the central department, where he thought he could get a footing, and rally a formidable force, before the government troops could reach him. But, when five days out, Lopez discovered that the Pampero was short of coal; as no time could be spared to remedy this deficiency, he resolved to effect a landing at once, and send back the Pampero for reïnforcements and supplies. At Key West he obtained favorable intelligence from Cuba, which confirmed his previous plans. He learned that a large portion of the troops had been sent to the eastern department; and he accordingly steered for Bahia Honda (deep bay). The current of the gulf, acting while the machinery of the boat was temporarily stopped for repairs, and the variation of the compass in the neighbor-

hood of so many arms, caused the steamer to run out of her
course on the night of the 10th; and when the morning broke, the invaders found themselves heading for the
narrow entrance of the harbor of Havana!

The course of the steamer was instantly altered; but
all on board momentarily expected the apparition of a war
steamer from the channel between the Moro and the Punta.
It appeared, afterwards, that the Pampero was signalized as
a strange steamer, but not reported as suspicious until
evening. The Pampero then made for the bay of Cabañas;
but, just as she was turning into the entrance, a Spanish
frigate and sloop-of-war were seen at anchor, the first of
which immediately gave chase, but, the wind failing, the
frigate gave it up, and returned to the bay to send intelligence of the expedition to Havana. The landing was finally
effected at midnight, between the 11th and 12th of August,
and the steamer was immediately sent off to the United
States for further reïnforcements. As it was necessary to
obtain transportation for the baggage, General Lopez
resolved to leave Col. Crittenden with one hundred and
twenty men to guard it, and with the remainder of the
expedition to push on to Las Pozas, a village about ten
miles distant, whence he could send back carts and horses
to receive it. Among the baggage were four barrels of
powder, two of cartridges, the officers' effects, including the
arms of the general, and the flag of the expedition. From

the powder and arms they should not have separated, but have divided that, against contingency.

In the mean time, seven picked companies of Spanish troops of the line had been landed at Bahia Honda, which force was strengthened by contingents drawn from the neighborhood. The march of the invading band to Las Pozas was straggling and irregular. On reaching the village, they found it deserted by the inhabitants. A few carts were procured and sent back to Crittenden, that he might advance with the baggage. Lopez here learned from a countryman of the preparations making to attack him. It was no portion of his plan to bring the men into action with regular troops, in their present undisciplined state; he proposed rather to take a strong position in the mountains, and there plant his standard as a rallying-point, and await the rising of the Cubans, and the return of the Pampero with reïnforcements for active operations.

As soon as Lopez learned the news from Bahia Honda, he despatched a peremptory order to Crittenden to hasten up with the rear-guard, abandoning the heavy baggage, but bringing off the cartridges and papers of the expedition.

But the fatal delay of Crittenden separated him forever from the main body, only a small detachment of his comrades (under Captain Kelly) ever reaching it. The next day, while breakfast was being prepared for them, the soldiers of the expedition were suddenly informed, by a volley from one of the houses of the village, that the Spanish troops were upon them. They flew to arms at once, and the Cuban company dislodged the vanguard of the enemy, who had fired, at the point of the bayonet, their captain, Oberto, receiving his death-wound in the spirited affair. General Enna, a brave officer, in command of the Spanish troops, made two charges in column on the centre of the invaders' line, but was repulsed by that deadly fire which is the preëminent characteristic of American troops. Four men alone escaped from the company heading the first column, and seventeen from that forming the advance of the second column of attack. The Spaniards were seized with a panic, and fled.

Lopez's force in this action amounted to about two hundred and eighty men; the Spaniards had more than eight hundred. The total loss of the former, in killed and wounded, was thirty-five; that of the latter, about two hundred men killed, and a large number wounded! The invaders landed with about eighty rounds of cartridges each; the Spanish dead supplied them with about twelve thousand more; and a further supply was subsequently obtained at Las Frias; the ammunition left with Crittenden was never recovered. In the battle of Las Pozas, General Enna's horse was shot under him, and his second in command killed. The invaders lost Colonel Downman, a brave American officer; while General Pragay was wounded, and afterwards died in consequence. Though the invaders fired well and did terrible execution, they could not be prevailed upon to charge the enemy, and gave great trouble to the officers by their insubordination. The night after the battle, Captain Kelly came up with forty men, and announced that the Spanish troops had succeeded in dividing the rearguard, and that the situation of Crittenden was unknown. It was not until some days afterwards that it was ascertained that Crittenden's party, attempting to leave the island in launches, had been made prisoners by a Spanish man-of-war. They were taken to Havana, and brutally shot at the castle of Atares.

About two o'clock on the 14th of August, the expedition resumed its march for the interior, leaving behind their wounded, who were afterwards killed and mutilated by the Spaniards. The second action with the Spanish troops occurred at the coffee-plantation of Las Frias, General Enna attacking with four howitzers, one hundred and twenty cavalry, and twelve hundred infantry. The Spanish general attacked with his cavalry, but they were met by a deadly fire, thrown into utter confusion, and forced to retreat, carrying off the general mortally wounded. The panic of the cavalry communicated itself to the infantry, and the result was a complete rout. This was the work of about two hundred muskets; for many of Lopez's men had thrown away their arms on the long and toilsome march.

The expedition, however, was too weak to profit by their desperate successes, and had no means of following up these victories. Plunging into the mountains, they wandered about for days, drenched with rain, destitute of food or

proper clothing, until despair at last seized them.   They separated from each other, a few steadfast comrades remaining
by their leader.   In the neighborhood of San Cristoval,
Lopez finally surrendered to a party of pursuers.   He was
treated with every indignity by his captors, though he sub-
mitted to everything with courage and serenity.   He was
taken in a steamer from Mariel to Havana.

Arrived here, he earnestly desired to obtain an interview
with Concha, who had been an old companion-in-arms with
him in Spain; not that he expected pardon at his hands,
but hoping to obtain a change in the manner of his death.
His soul shrank from the infamous *garrotte*, and he aspired
to the indulgence of the *cuatro tiros* (four shots).   Both
the interview and the indulgence were refused, and he was
executed on the first of September, at seven o'clock in the
morning, in the Punta, by that mode of punishment which
the Spaniards esteem the most infamous of all.   When he
landed at Bahia Honda, he stooped and kissed the earth,
with the fond salutation, " *Querida Cuba* " (dear Cuba) !
and his last words, pronounced in a tone of deep tenderness,
were, " *Muero por mi amada Cuba* " (I die for my beloved Cuba).*

The remainder of the prisoners who fell into the hands
of the authorities were sent to the Moorish fortress of Ceu-

* General Lopez was born in Venezuela, South America, in 1798 ; and
hence, at the time of his execution, must have been about fifty-two years
of age.   He early became an adopted citizen of Cuba, and espoused one
of its daughters.

ta; but Spain seems to have been ashamed of the massacre of Atares, and has atoned for the ferocity of her colonial officials by leniency towards the misguided men of the expedition, granting them a pardon.

At present it may be said that "order reigns in Warsaw," and· the island is comparatively quiet in the presence of a vast armed force. To Concha have succeeded Canedo and Pezuelas, but no change for the better has taken place in the administration of the island. Rigorous to the native population, insolent and overbearing to foreigners, respecting no flag and regarding no law, the captains-general bear themselves as though Spain was still a first-rate power as of yore, terrible on land, and afloat still the mistress of the sea.

5*

CHAPTER IV.

Present condition of Cuba — Secret treaty with France and England — British plan for the Africanization of the island — Sale of Cuba — Measures of General Pezuela — Registration of slaves — Intermarriage of blacks and whites — Contradictory proclamations — Spanish duplicity — A Creole's view of the crisis and the prospect.

CUBA is at present politically in a critical and alarming condition, and the most intelligent natives and resident foreigners live in constant dread of a convulsion more terrific and sanguinary than that which darkened the annals of St. Domingo. Those best informed of the temper, designs and position of Spain, believe in the existence of a secret treaty between that country, France and England, by which the two latter powers guarantee to Spain her perpetual possession of the island, on condition of her carrying out the favorite abolition schemes of the British government, and Africanizing the island. Spain, it is supposed, unable to stand alone, and compelled to elect between the loss of her colony and subserviency to her British ally, has chosen of the two evils that which wounds her pride the least, and is best calculated to secure the interests of monarchical Europe. All the recent measures of the Captain-general Pezuela are calculated to produce the conviction that the Africanization of Cuba has been resolved upon; and, if his alarming proclamation of the third of May has been somewhat modified by subsequent proclamations and official declarations, it is only because the Spanish government lacks the boldness to unmask all its schemes, while the Eastern war prevents France and Great Britain from sending large armaments to Cuba to support it; and because the national vessels and troops destined to swell the government forces in the island have not all arrived. But for the existence of the war in the East, the manifestoes of the captain-general would have been much more explicit. As it is, they are sufficiently bold and menacing.

A peaceful solution to the question of Cuba, by its sale to the United States, is not regarded as probable by the best-informed Creoles. They say that, even if the queen were disposed to sell the island, it would be impossible to obtain the consent of the Cortes. The integrity of the Spanish domain, including all the islands, is protected by legal enactment; and it would require the abrogation of a fundamental law before it could be consummated.* Now, the Spanish subjects well understand that they would not be likely to be gainers by the sale of Cuba, however large a

---

* The administration of Bravo Murillo fell in an attempt of this kind, and did not rise again.

sum the United States might be willing to pay for it, while the monopoly to trade, the bestowal of lucrative insular offices on Spaniards alone, and other incidental advantages, give them a direct interest in the maintenance of the present order of things. Those who take this view of the question say that if Spain has not promptly rejected the overtures supposed to have been made by our minister at Madrid, this delay indicates only a conscious weakness, and not any hesitation of purpose. It is simply a diplomatic trick — a temporizing policy. Why, they ask, if Spain had any idea of parting with the island, would she be making naval and military preparations on a grand and costly scale, at home, while in the island she is making large levies, and enrolling colored troops, not as militia, as the government has falsely given out, but as regulars? We are reluctant to abandon the hope of our purchasing the island, but candor compels us to state the plausible arguments of those who assert that no success can possibly attend the plan for its peaceable acquisition.

Within a brief space of time, the administration of General Pezuela has been signalized by measures of great significance and importance : The decree of the third of May; the order for the registration of slaves introduced into the island in violation of the treaty of 1817 ; the decree freeing more than fifteen thousand *emancipados* in the space of a fortnight; that of May 25th, enrolling and arming negroes and mulattoes; the project for importing negroes and mulattoes from Africa, under the name of free apprentices; the institution of free schools for the instruction of the blacks, while the whites are abandoned to their own resources; and, finally, the legalization of the intermarriages of blacks and whites, which last measure has actually been carried into effect, to the indignation of the Creoles,— all these measures show the determination of the Spanish government to bring about the emancipation of slavery, and the social equalization of the colored and white population, that it may maintain its grasp upon the island, under penalty of a war of races, which could only terminate in the extinction of the whites, in case of a revolutionary movement.

The proclamation of the third of May, alluded to above, and disclosing some of the abolition plans of the government, produced a startling sensation. In it the captain-general said: "It is time for the planter to substitute for the rapid but delusive advantages derived from the sale of human flesh, safer profits, more in harmony with civilization, religion and morals;" and that "the time had come to make the life of the slave sweeter than that of the white man who labors under another name in Europe." The proclamation, coupled with that conferring exclusive educational advantages on colored persons, roused even the Spaniards; some of the wealthiest and most influential of whom held secret meetings to discuss the measures to be adopted in such a crisis, in which it was resolved to withhold all active aid from the government, some going so far

as to advocate the making of common cause with the
Creoles. The mere hint of a fusion between the Spaniards
and Creoles, whom it has been the policy of the colonial
government to alienate from each other, was sufficient to excite the fears of the captain-general ; and accordingly, on the
31st of May, he published a sort of explanatory manifesto,
designed to allay the alarm of the Spaniards, and conflict-
ing, in several points, with that of the 3d. "Her Majesty's government," says the document of the 31st, " is well
aware that the unhappy race (the Africans), once placed
among civilized men, and protected by the religion and the
great laws of our ancestors, is, in its so-called slavery, a
thousand times happier than other European classes, whose
liberty is only nominal." If this assertion were true, what
becomes of the famous declaration, in the former proclamation, that the time had arrived to make the life of the slave
happier than of the white European laborer ? If this assertion were true, that " good time " had not only arrived, but
passed away, and his measures for the improvement of the
involuntary bondmen were actually supererogatory. The
owners of slaves are, moreover, assured that they shall not
be disturbed in the possession of their " legitimate property," and that the government will conciliate a due regard
for such property " with the sacred fulfilment of treaties."

It is very evident that the Creoles are doomed to be the
victims of Spanish duplicity. It is notorious that many
thousands of slaves have been introduced into the island, for

a series of years, with the connivance of the government, when they had it in their power, at any time, to stop the traffic altogether. The vigilance of the British cruisers was baffled by the assurance that the Africans thus brought over were apprentices, Spain never hesitating to deceive an ally; and now, when compelled to keep faith, in a desperate emergency, she betrays her own subjects, and throws the penalty of her own bad faith on them.

A gentleman residing in Cuba writes: "No one can be here, and watch the progress of things, without being convinced that the ultimate object is the emancipation of the slaves of the island transported subsequent to the treaty of 1820, which will comprise four-fifths of the whole number; and no one who is an attentive observer, and with his ears open, but must be satisfied that there is some other powerful influence brought to bear on the subject besides Spain. Take, for instance, the late order for the registration of the slaves. The British consul openly says that the British government have been, for a long time, urging the measure. But it is not only in this, but in every other step taken, that the British finger is constantly seen. A thousand corroborative circumstances could be cited. Cuba is to-day indebted to Russia for being free from this calamity. But for the emperor's obstinacy, there would have been an English and French fleet that would have enabled them to carry out all the measures they have in contemplation."

With relation to the intermarriage of blacks and whites,

our informant says, "Many marriages have been performed
since the date of the circular," — that of the Bishop of
Havana to the curates of the island, by the authority of
the captain-general.

"The captain-general," says the same authority, "is
now exerting his influence for the admission of blacks into
the university, to prepare them for clerical orders. Should
this system be adopted, I fear it will lead to bad consequences. It will, of course, be strenuously opposed. The
indignation of the Creoles has been difficult to restrain,—
at which you cannot be surprised, when their daughters,
wives and sisters, are daily insulted, particularly by those
in uniform. I fear a collision may take place. If once
commenced, it will be terrific."

The decree authorizing the celebration of marriages
between blacks and whites has probably produced more
indignation among the Creoles than any other official acts
of the captain-general. It was directed to the bishop in
the form of a circular, and issued on the 22d of May. On
the 29th of the same month, the bishop transmitted copies
of it to all the curates within his jurisdiction; and, as we
have seen, many of these incongruous marriages have been
already solemnized. Notwithstanding these notorious and
well-authenticated facts, the official organ of the government, the *Diario de la Marina*, had the effrontery to
publish a denial of the transaction, asserting it to be mere

idle gossip, without the slightest foundation, and ridiculing the idea in a tone of levity and *persiflage*.

This may teach us how little dependence is to be placed on the declarations of the Spanish officials; and we shall be prepared to receive with incredulity the denial, in the name of the queen, of the existence of a treaty with England, having for its base the abolition of slavery, as a reward for British aid in preserving Cuba to Spain. The captain-general says that she relies not on foreign aid to maintain her rights, but on her powerful " navy and disciplined army; on the loyalty of the very immense (*inmensisima*) majority of her vigorous native citizens (Creoles); on the strength imparted to the good by the defence of their hearths, their laws and their God; and on the hurricanes and yellow fever for the enemy."

" Here," writes a Cuban gentleman, commenting on the above declaration, " we must make a pause, and remark, *en passant*, that the name of her majesty thus invoked, far from giving force to the denial, weakens it greatly; for we all know the value of the royal word, particularly that of her majesty Isabella II. In her name a full pardon was offered to Armenteros and his associates, who raised the cry of independence in Trinidad, and this document effected the purpose for which it was designed. Armenteros and the others, who placed reliance in the royal word, were, some of them, shot, and the rest deported to African dungeons. No reliance can be placed on the loyalty of the vast majority of the vigorous citizens (unless the negroes alone are comprehended under this phrase), when the whites are deprived of arms for the defence of their country, and men are fined five pesos for carrying canes of a larger size than can be readily introduced into a gun-barrel, and free people of color are alone admitted into the ranks of the troops. The Cubans are not relied upon, since, to prevent their joining Lopez, all the roads were blockaded, and everybody found on them shot; and the immense number of exiles does not prove the majority which favors the government to be so prodigious.

"The value of the powerful navy and well-trained army of the island was shown in the landing of Lopez, and the victories that three hundred men constantly obtained over an army of seven thousand, dispersing only when ammunition failed them. Hurricanes and the yellow fever are most melancholy arms of defence; and, if they only injured the enemy, the Spaniards, who are as much exposed as other Europeans to the fatal influence, would be the true enemies of Cuba."

The following remarks on the present condition and prospects of the island are translated from a letter written by an intelligent Creole, thoroughly conversant with its affairs:

"The whites tremble for their existence and property; no one thinks himself secure; confidence has ceased, and with it credit; capitalists have withdrawn their money from circulation; the banks of deposit have suspended their discounts; premiums have reached a fabulous point for the best of paper. The government was not ignorant that this would be the result, and prepared to get out of the momentary crisis by the project of a bank,* published in the *Gaceta* of the 4th (May); but the most needy class, in the present embarrassed circumstances, is that of the planters; and it is necessary, to enable them to fulfil their engagements, that their notes should be made payable at the end of the year,— that is, from harvest to harvest,— and not at the end of six months, as provided for in the regulations. But it matters not; we are pursuing the path which will precipitate us into the abyss, if instantaneous and efficacious help does not come to save the island from the imminent ruin which threatens it.

" The cause of the liberty of nations has always perished in its cradle, because its defenders have never sought to deviate from legal paths,— because they have followed the principles sanctioned by the laws of nations; while despots, always the first to exact obedience to them when it suited their convenience, have been the first to infringe them when they came into collision with their interests. Their alliances to suppress liberty are called *holy*, and the crimes they commit by invading foreign territories, and summoning foreign troops to their aid to oppress their own vassals, are sacred duties, compliances with secret compacts; and, if the

---

* Pezuela's bank is to have a capital of two million dollars; the government to be a shareholder for half a million. The effect of such an institution would be to drain the island of specie.

congresses, parliaments and Cortes of other nations, raise
the cry to Heaven, they answer, the government has protested,— acts have been performed without their sanction,—
there is no remedy,— they are acts accomplished.

"An act accomplished will shortly be the abolition of
slavery in Cuba; and the tardy intervention of the United
States will only have taken place when its brilliant constel-
lation lights up the vast sepulchre which will cover the
bodies of her sons, sacrificed to the black race as a reward
for their sympathies with American institutions, and the
vast carnage it will cost to punish the African victors.
What can be done to-day without great sacrifices to help
the Cubans, to-morrow cannot be achieved without the
effusion of rivers of blood, and when the few surviving
Cubans will curse an intervention which, deaf to their cries,
will only be produced by the cold calculations of egotism.
Then the struggle will not be with the Spaniards alone.
The latter will now accede to all the claims of the cabinet
at Washington, by the advice of the ambassadors of France
and England, to advance, meanwhile, with surer step to
the end,— to give time for the solution of the Eastern question, and for France and England to send their squadrons
into these waters. Well may they deny the existence of
secret treaties; this is very easy for kings, as it will be
when the case of the present treaty comes up, asserting that
the treaty was posterior to their negative, or refusing expla-
nations as inconsistent with their dignity. But we witness

the realization of our fears; we see the Spanish government imperturbably setting on foot plans which were thought to be the delirium of excited imaginations; doing at once what promised to be a gradual work; and hear it declared, by distinguished persons, who possess the confidence of General Pezuela, that the existence of the treaty is certain, and that the United States will be told that they should have accepted the offer made to become a party to it, in which case the other two powers could not have adopted the abolition scheme. But, supposing this treaty to have no existence, the fact of the abolition of slavery is no less certain. It is only necessary to read the proclamation of the captain-general, if the last acts of the government be not sufficiently convincing. The result to the island of Cuba, and to the United States is the same, either way. If the latter do not hasten to avert the blow, they will soon find it impossible to remedy the evil. In the island there is not a reflecting man,— foreigner or native, Creole or European,— who does not tremble for the future that awaits us, at a period certainly not far remote."

6*

CHAPTER V.

HAVING thus briefly glanced at the political story of Cuba, let us now pass to a consideration of such peculiarities of climate, soil and population, as would naturally interest a stranger on visiting the island. The form, geographically speaking, of Cuba, is quite irregular, and resembles the blade of a Turkish scimeter slightly curved back, or approaching the form of a long, narrow crescent. It stretches away in this shape from east to west, throwing its western end into a curve, as if to form an impregnable barrier to the outlet of the Gulf of Mexico; and as if, at some ancient period, it had formed a part of the American continent, and had been severed on its north side from the Florida peninsula by the wearing of the Gulf-stream, and from Yucatan, on its south-western point, by a current setting into the gulf.

Its political position all concede to be of the most vital importance to the United States; and this will be apparent to any one, from the slightest inspection of the map.

It is the most westerly of the West Indian isles, and, compared with the rest, has nearly twice as much superficial extent of territory. Its greatest extent, from east to west, is about six hundred miles; its narrowest part, twenty-two miles. The circumference is about two thousand miles, containing some thirty-two thousand square miles.* The narrow form of the island, and the Cordillera chain of mountains, which divides it throughout its whole length, leave a very limited course for its rivers and streams; and consequently these in the rainy season become torrents, and during the rest of the year are nearly dried up. Those that sustain themselves throughout the year are well stocked with delicate and finely-flavored fish.

Probably no place on the earth has a finer or more desirable climate than has the main portion of Cuba; † with the clear atmosphere of the low latitudes, no mist, the sun seldom obscured, and the appearance of the stars and sky at night far brighter and more beautiful than at the north.‡ The atmosphere does not seem to lose its transpar-

---

* Humboldt's calculation makes it contain forty-three thousand, three hundred and eighty square miles ; but other estimates approximate more nearly our own statement.

† According to Dr. Finlay, a resident physician on the island, its hottest months are July and August, when the mean temperature is from 80° to 83° Fahrenheit.

‡ "The nights are very dark, but the darkness is as if transparent ; the air is not felt. There could not be more beautiful nights in Paradise." — *Miss Bremer's Letters.*

ency with the departure of day. Sunset is ever remarkable for its soft, mellow beauty here, and the long twilight that follows it. For many years the island has been the resort of the northern invalid in search of health, especially of those laboring under pulmonary affections; the soft, soothing power of the climate having a singularly healing influence, as exercised in the balmy trade-winds.* The climate so uniformly soft and mild, the vegetation so thriving and beautiful, the fruits so delicious and abundant, seem to give it a character almost akin to that we have seen described in tales of fairy land.

The declining health of a beloved companion was the motive which induced the author of these pages to visit the delightful climate of Cuba, with the hope that its genial and kindly influence might revive her physical powers; nor were these hopes disappointed; for, transplanted from the rough climate of our own New England, immediate and permanent improvement was visible. To persons in the early stages of pulmonary complaints the West Indies hold forth great promise of relief; and, at the period when invalid New Englanders most require to avoid their own homes, namely, during the prevailing east winds of April, May and June, the island of Cuba is in the glory of high summer, and enjoying the healthiest period of its yearly returns. After the early part of June, the unacclimated would do

---

* When consumption *originates* in Cuba, it runs its course so rapidly that there is, perhaps, no wonder the Creoles should deem it, as they universally do, to be contagious.

well to take passage up the gulf to New Orleans, and come gradually north with the advancing season. From the proximity of Cuba in the north-western parts to our own continent, the climate is variable, and a few hundred feet above the level of the sea ice is sometimes formed, but snow never falls upon the island, though it is occasionally visited in this region by hail storms. In the cities and near the swamps, the yellow fever, that scourge of all hot climates, prevails from the middle of June to the last of October; but in the interior of the island, where the visitor is at a wholesome distance from humidity and stagnant water, it is no more unhealthy than our own cities in summer. It is doubtful if Havana, even in the fever season, is as unhealthy as New Orleans during the same period of the year.

The principal cities of the island are Havana, with a population of about two hundred thousand; Matanzas, twenty-five thousand; Puerto Principe, fourteen thousand; Santiago de Cuba, thirty thousand; Trinidad, thirteen thousand; St. Salvador, eight thousand; Manzanilla, three thousand; Cardenas, Nuevitas, Sagua la Grande, Mariel, etc. etc. Cuba abounds in fine large harbors; those of Havana, Niepe and Nuevitas, are among the best. The bay of Matanzas is also capacious; Cardenas and the roadstead of Sagua la Grande have plenty of water for brigs and schooners. Matanzas,* though second to Puerto Principe

---

* The first lines of this city were traced on Saturday, the 10th of October, 1693, by Señor Manzaneda, under whose government it was founded. It was named San Cárlos Alcázar de Matanzas; the last word, that by which it is known, signifying the slaughter of a battle-field.

in point of inhabitants, yet stands next to Havana in commercial importance, and is said to be much healthier than the capital. It is located in a valley in one of the most fertile portions of the island, the city extending from the flat sea-shore up to the picturesque and verdant heights by which the town is surrounded in the form of an amphitheatre. The fortifications are of rather a meagre character. The custom-house is the most prominent building which strikes the eye on approaching the city by water, and is an elegant structure of stone, but one story high, built at the early part of the present century. On the heights above the city, the inhabitants have planted their country seats, and from the bay the whole scene is most delightfully picturesque. There are two fine churches in Matanzas, and a second-class theatre, cockpit, etc. Statistics show the custom-house receipts of the port to exceed the large sum of a million and a half dollars annually. Besides the railroad leading to Havana, there is another leading to the interior and bearing southward, of some thirty or forty miles in length. On all the Cuban railroads you ride in American-built cars, drawn by American-built engines, and conducted by American engineers. The back country from Matanzas is rich in sugar and coffee plantations.

Puerto Principe is the capital of the central department of the island, and is situated in the interior. The trade of the place, from the want of water-carriage, is inconsiderable, and bears no proportion to the number of inhabitants. What over portion of the produce of Puerto Principe and its immediate neighborhood is exported, must find its way first to Nuevitas, twelve and a half leagues distant, from whence it is shipped, and from whence it receives in return its foreign supplies. It is situated about one hundred and fifty miles from Havana. Its original locality, when founded by Velasquez, was Nuevitas, but the inhabitants, when the place was feeble in numbers and strength, were forced to remove to this distance inland, to avoid the fierce incursions of the Buccaneers, who thronged the coast.

Santiago de Cuba has a noble harbor, and is defended by a miniature Moro Castle, being a well-planned fortress after the same style, and known as *El Moro*. This city was founded in 1512, and is the capital of the eastern department of the island, but has at various times suffered severely from earthquakes, and within a couple of years was visited by the cholera, which swept off some five or six thousand of its population in about the same number of weeks. Santiago, though it now presents many features of decay, and its cathedral is closed for fear of disaster occurring if it should be occupied, is yet the third city on the island in a commercial point of view. The immediate neighborhood of the city being mountainous and somewhat sterile, produces little sugar, but the many fine coffee estates, and several vast copper mines of uncomputed extent and value, which have been worked by English companies, give it much importance. It is two hundred and thirty leagues from Havana, on the south coast.

Trinidad, situated about a league from Casilda, on the south coast, and ninety miles from Havana, is probably one of the healthiest and pleasantest locations for invalids on the island. It lies at the base of a ridge of mountains that protect it from the north wind, and is free from all humidity, with that great blessing, good water, at hand, an article which unfortunately is very scarce in Cuba.

Our first view of Moro Castle was gained from the quarter-deck, after a fifteen days' voyage; it was just as the sun was dipping into the sea, too late for us to enter the harbor, for the rules of the port are rigorously observed, and we were obliged to stand off and on through the night. At early morning our jack was set at the fore as a signal for a pilot, and at noon we had answered the rough peremptory hail from the castle, and dropped anchor in the safe and beautiful harbor of the capital. The scene was absorbingly interesting to a stranger. Around us floated the flags of many nations, conspicuous among which were the gallant stars and stripes. On the one side lay the city, on a low, level plain, while the hills that make the opposite side of the harbor presented a beautiful picture of the soft green sward and the luxuriant verdure that forms the constant garb of the tropics.

As Paris is said to be France, so is Havana Cuba, and its history embraces in no small degree that of all the island, being the centre of its talent, wealth and population. Every visible circumstance proclaims the great importance of the city, even to the most casual observer. Moro Castle * frowning over the narrow entrance of the harbor, the strong battery answering to it on the opposite point, and known as La Punta, the long range of cannon and barracks on the city side, the powerful and massive fortress of the Cabanas † crowning the hill behind the Moro, all speak unitedly of the immense importance of the place. Havana is the heart of Cuba, and will never be yielded unless the whole island be given up; indeed, the possessors of this strong-hold command the whole Spanish West Indies. The bay, shaped like an outspread hand, the wrist for the entrance, is populous with the ships of all nations,‡ and the city, with its 200,000 inhabitants, is a depot of wealth and luxury. With an enormous extent of public buildings, cathedrals, antique and venerable churches and convents, with the palaces of nobles and private gentlemen of wealth, all render this capital of Cuba probably the richest place for its number of square rods in the world.

Beside the Royal University of Havana, a medical and law school, and chairs on all the natural sciences, it contains many other institutions of learning. It is true that, in spite

* Moro Castle was first built in 1633; the present structure was erected on the ruins of the first, destroyed by the English in 1762.

† Built by Charles III., and said to have cost the sum of $7,000,000. According to Rev. L. L. Allen's lecture on Cuba, it was more than forty years in building.

‡ The port of Havana is one of the best harbors in the world. It has a very narrow entrance, but spreads immediately into a vast basin, embracing the whole city, and large enough to hold a thousand ships of war. — *Alexander H. Everett.*

of their liberal purpose and capability, there is a blight, as it were, hanging over them all. Pupils enlist cautiously, suffer undue restraint, and in spite of themselves seem to feel that there is an unseen influence at work against the spirit of these advantages. Among the schools are a Royal Seminary for girls, a free school of sculpture and painting, a mercantile school, also free, with many private institutions of learning, of course not to be compared in ability or general advantages to like institutions with us. There is a fine museum of Natural History, and just outside the city walls a very extensive botanical garden. No one, even among the islanders, who would be supposed to feel the most pride in the subject, will for a moment deny, however, that the means for education are very limited in Cuba. An evidence of this is perceptibly evinced by the fact that the sons of the planters are almost universally sent abroad, mostly to this country, for educational purposes. An order was not long since promulgated, by direction of the home government, in which the inhabitants are forbidden to send their children to the United States, for the purpose of education. A bold, decided order.

Of course the reason for this is quite apparent, and is openly acknowledged in Havana, viz: — that these youths, during their residence here, adopt liberal ideas and views of our republican policy, which become fixed principles with them ; nor is there any doubt of this being the case, for such students as have thus returned, unhesitatingly (among friends) avow their sentiments, and most ardently express a hope for Cuban independence ; and this class, too, upon the island are far more numerous than might at first be supposed. Those who have been educated in France, Germany, and England, seem at once to imbibe the spirit of those youths who have returned from the United States, and long before there was any open demonstration relative to the first Lopéz expedition, these sons of the planters had formed themselves into a secret society, which is doubtless still sustained, with the avowed purpose of exercising its ability and means to free Cuba, sooner or later, from the Spanish yoke.

The city of Havana is surrounded by a high wall and ditch, and its gates are always strictly guarded by soldiery, no stranger being permitted to pass unchallenged. The streets, which are extremely narrow, are all Macadamized, and cross each other at right angles, like those of Philadelphia and some other American cities. There are no sidewalks, unless a narrow line of flag-stones which are level with the surface of the street may be so called. Indeed, the people have little use for sidewalks, for they drive almost universally about town in place of walking, being thus borne about in that peculiar vehicle, a volante. A woman of respectability is never seen on foot in the streets, and this remark, as singular as it may sound to our Broadway and Washington-street belles, is applicable even to the humblest classes ; unless, indeed, it be the fruit women from the country, with their baskets richly laden upon their heads,

while they cry the names of their tempting burdens in the
long drawling Spanish style.

The architecture of the city houses is exceedingly heavy,
giving to them an appearance of great age. They are constructed so as almost universally to form squares in their
centres, which constitutes the only yard which the house
can have, and upon which the lofty arches of the corridor
look down. The lower story is always occupied as store-
room, kitchen, and stable, (think of a suite of drawing-rooms
over a stable!) while the universal volante blocks up in
part the only entrance to the house. From this inner
court-yard a wide flight of steps leads to the second story,
from the corridor of which all the rooms open, giving them
an opening front and rear on two sides at least. As peculiar as this mode of building may seem, it is nevertheless
well adapted to the climate, and one becomes exceedingly
well satisfied with the arrangement.

An air of rude grandeur reigns over all the structure,
the architecture being mainly Gothic and Saracenic. The
rooms are all lofty, and the floors are stuccoed or tiled,
while the walls and ceilings are frequently ornamented in
fresco, the excellence of the workmanship of course varying
in accordance with the owner's or occupant's means, and
his ability to procure an artist of high or *mediocre* talent.
But the most striking peculiarity of the town house in
Cuba, is the great care taken to render it safe against
assault. Every man's house is literally his castle here.

each accessible window being barricaded with iron bars, while large massive folding doors secure the entrance to the house, being bullet proof and of immense strength. No carpets are seen here, and from the neighboring Isle of Pines, which lies off the southern shore of Cuba, a thick slate is found, also marble and jasper of various colors, which are cut in squares, and form the general material for floors in the dwelling-houses. The heat of the climate renders carpets, or even wooden floors, quite insupportable, and they are very rarely to be found.

We have said that the Creole ladies never stir abroad except in the national volante, and whatever their domestic habits may be, they are certainly, in this respect, good *housekeepers*. A Cuban belle could never, we fancy, be made to understand the pleasures of that most profitless of all employments, spinning street-yarn. While our ladies are busily engaged in sweeping the sidewalks of Chestnut-street and Broadway with their silk flounces, she wisely leaves that business to the gangs of criminals who perform the office with their limbs chained, and a ball attached to preserve their equilibrium. It is perhaps in part owing to these habits that the feet of the Cuban señorita are such a marvel of smallness and delicacy, seemingly made rather for ornament than for use. She knows the charm of the *petit pied bien chaussé* that delights the Parisian, and accordingly, as you catch a glimpse of it, as she steps into the volante, you perceive that it is daintily shod in a French slipper, the

7*

sole of which is scarcely more substantial in appearance than writing paper.*

The feet of the Havana ladies are made for ornament and for dancing. Though with a roundness of figure that leaves nothing to be desired in symmetry of form, yet they are light as a sylph, clad in muslin and lace, so languid and light that it would seem as if a breeze might waft them away like a summer cloud. They are passionately fond of dancing, and tax the endurance of the gentlemen in their heroic worship of Terpsichore. Inspired by the thrilling strains of those Cuban airs, which are at once so sweet and brilliant, they glide or whirl through the mazes of the dance hour after hour, until daylight breaks upon the scene of fairy revel. Then, "exhausted but not satiated," they betake themselves to sleep, to dream of the cadences of some Cuban Strauss, and to beat time in imagination to the lively notes, and to dream over the soft words and winning glances they have exchanged.

Beautiful as eastern houris, there is a striking and endearing charm about the Cuban ladies, their very motion being replete with a native grace; every limb elastic and supple. Their voices are sweet and low, "an excellent thing in woman," and the subdued tone of their complexions is relieved by the arch vivacity of night-black eyes that alternately

---

* "Her hands and feet are as small and delicate as those of a child. She wears the finest satin slippers, with scarcely any soles, which, luckily, are never destined to touch the street." — *Countess Merlin's Letters.*

swim in melting lustre or sparkle in expressive glances. Their costume is never ostentatious, though costly; the most delicate muslin, the finest linen, the richest silk, the most exquisitely made satin shoes, — these, of course, render their chaste attire exceedingly expensive. There are no " strong-minded " women among them, nor is it hardly possible to conceive of any extremity that could induce them to get up a woman's right convention — a suspension of fans and volantes might produce such a phenomenon, but we very much doubt it.

The Creole ladies lead a life of decided ease and pleasure. What little work they do is very light and lady-like, a little sewing or embroidery; the bath and the *siesta* divide the sultry hours of the day. They wait until nearly sun-set for the drive in the dear volante, and then go to respond by sweet smiles to the salutations of the *caballeros* on the Paseoes, and after the long twilight to the Plaza de Armas, to listen to the governor's military band, and then perhaps to join the mazy dance. Yet they are capable of deep and high feeling, and when there was a prospect of the liberation of the island, these fair patriots it will be remembered gave their most precious jewels and ornaments as a contribution to the glorious cause of liberty.

CHAPTER VI.

ON no occasion is the difference between the manners of a Protestant and Catholic community so strongly marked as on the Sabbath. In the former, a sober seriousness stamps the deportment of the people, even when they are not engaged in devotional exercises ; in the latter, worldly pleasures and religious exercises are pursued as it were at the same time, or follow each other in incongruous succession. The Parisian flies from the church to the railway station, to take a pleasure excursion into the country, or passes with careless levity from St. Genevieve to the Jardin Mabille ; in New Orleans, the Creole, who has just bent his knee before the altar, repairs to the French opera, and the Cuban from the blessing of the priest to the parade in the Plaza. Even the Sunday ceremonial of the church is a pageant; the splendid robe of the officiating priest, changed in the course of the offices, like the costumes of actors in a drama; the music, to Protestant ears operatic and exciting; the clouds of incense that scatter their intoxicating perfumes; the chants in a strange tongue, unknown to the mass of worshippers;— all these give the services a holiday and carnival character.*

Far be it from us to charge these congregations with any undue levity ; many a lovely Creole kneels upon the marble floor, entirely estranged from the brilliant groups around her, and unconscious for the time of the admiration she excites; many a *caballero* bows in reverence, forgetful, for the time being, of the bright eyes that are too often the load-star of attraction to the church; and there are very many who look beyond the glittering symbols to the great truths and the great Being they are intended to typify. But we fear that a large portion of the community who thus worship, attach more importance to the representation than to the principles or things represented. The impression made by the Sabbath ceremonies of the church strikes us as evanescent, and as of such a character as to be at once obliterated by the excitement of the worldly pleasures that follow. Still, if the Sabbath in Catholic countries be not wholly devoted to religious observances, neither are the week days wholly absorbed by business and pleasure. The churches and chapels are always open, silently but elo-

---

* The influence of fifteen minutes in the church, if salutary, seems soon dissipated by the business and amusements without its walls. The shops are open ; the cock-pit fuller than on busier days of the week ; and the streets thronged with volantes ; the theatres and ball rooms crowded ; and the city devoted to pleasure.—*Rev. Abiel Abbot's Letters.*

quently inviting to devotion; and it is much to be able to
step aside, at any moment, from the temptations, business
and cares of life, into an atmosphere of seclusion and religion. The solemn quiet of an old cathedral on a week-
day is impressive from its very contrast with the tumult
outside.

Within its venerable walls the light seems chastened as it
falls through storied panes, and paints the images of Christian saints and martyrs on the cold pavement of the aisles.
Who can tell how many a tempest-tossed soul has found
relief and strength from the ability to withdraw itself at
once from the intoxicating whirl of the world and expand in
prayer in one of these hospitable and ever open sanctuaries ?
The writer is a firm Protestant, by education, by association
and feeling, but he is not so bigoted as not to see features
in the Catholic system worthy of commendation. Whether
the Catholic church has accomplished its mission, and exhausted its means of good, is a question open to discussion,
but that in the past it has achieved much for the cause of
true religion cannot be denied. Through the darkest period
in the history of the world, it was the lamp that guided to
a higher civilization, and the bulwark of the people against
the crushing force of feudalism ; and with all the objections
which it discovers to a Protestant eye, it still preserves many
beautiful customs.

The Sabbath in Havana breaks upon the citizens amid
the ringing of bells from the different convents and churches,

the firing of cannon from the forts and vessels, the noise of trumpets, and the roll of the drum.   Sunday is no day of physical rest here.   The stores are open as usual, the same cries are heard in the streets, and the lottery tickets are vended as ever at each corner.   The individual who devotes himself to this business rends the air with his cries of temptation to the passing throng, each one of whom he earnestly assures is certain to realize enormous pecuniary returns by the smallest investment, in tickets, or portions of tickets, which he holds in sheets, while he brandishes a huge pair of scissors, ready to cut in any desired proportion.   The day proves no check to the omnipresent "organ grinders," the monkey shows, and other characteristic scenes.   How unlike a New England Sabbath is all this, how discordant to the feelings of one who has been brought up amid our Puritanic customs of the sacred day !   And yet the people of Havana seem to be impressed with no small degree of reverence for the Catholic faith.   The rough Montero from the country, with his long line of loaded mules, respectfully raises his panama with one hand, while he makes the sign of the cross with the other, as he passes the church.   The calisero or postilion, who dashes by with his master in the volante, does not forget, in his hurry, to bend to the pommel of his saddle ; and even the little negro slave children may be observed to fold their arms across their breasts and remain reverentially silent until they have passed its doors.

The city abounds in beautifully arranged squares, ornamented by that king of the tropical forest, the Royal Palm, with here and there a few orange trees, surrounded by a luxuriant hedge of limes. The largest and most beautiful of these squares is the *Plaza de Armas*, fronting which is the Governor's palace, and about which are the massive stone barracks of the Spanish army. This square is surrounded by an iron railing and divided into beautiful walks, planted on either side with gaudy flowers, and shadowed by oranges and palms, while a grateful air of coolness is diffused around by the playing of a copious fountain into a large stone basin, surmounted by a marble statue of Ferdinand. Public squares, parks and gardens, are the lungs of great cities, and their value increases as the population becomes dense. Heap story upon story of costly marble, multiply magazines and palaces, yet neglect to provide, in their midst, some glimpse of nature, some opening for the light and air of heaven, and the costliest and most sumptuous of cities would prove but a dreary dwelling-place. The eye wearies, in time, of the glories of art, but of the gifts of nature never, and in public squares and gardens both may be happily combined.

Human culture brings trees, shrubs and flowers to their fullest development, fosters and keeps green the emerald sward, and brings the bright leaping waters into the midst of the graces of nature. Nowhere does a beautiful statue look more beautiful than when erected in a frame-work of deep foliage. These public squares are the most attractive

PLAZA DE ARMAS AND GOVERNOR'S PALACE.

features of cities.   Take from London Hyde Park, from
Paris the Champs Elysées and the Tuilleries gardens, the
Battery and the Park from New York, and the Common
from Boston, and they would be but weary wildernesses of
brick, stone and mortar.   The enlightened corporation that
bestows on a young city the gift of a great park, to be enjoyed in common forever, does more for posterity than if it
raised the most sumptuous columns and palaces for public
use or display.

The Plaza de Armas of Havana is a living evidence of
this, and is the nightly resort of all who can find time to be
there, while the governor's military band performs always
from seven to nine o'clock.   The Creoles call it "the poor
man's opera," it being free to all; every class resorts hither;
and even the ladies, leaving their volantes, sometimes walk
with husband or brother within the precincts of the Plaza.
We are told that "the man who has not music in his soul
is fit for treason, stratagem and spoils."   It is undoubtedly
from motives of policy that the Havanese authorities provide this entertainment for the people.   How ungrateful it
would be to overthrow a governor whose band performs such
delightful polkas, overtures and marches; and yet, it requires some circumspection for the band-master to select
airs for a Creole audience.   It would certainly never do to
give them "Yankee Doodle;" their sympathies with the
"*Norte Americanos*" are sufficiently lively without any
such additional stimulus; and it is well for the authorities

to have a care, for the power of national airs is almost incredible. It was found necessary, in the times of the old Bourbons, to forbid the performance of the "*Ranz des Vaches*," because it so filled the privates of the Swiss guards with memories of their native home that they deserted in numbers. The Scotch air of "Lochaber no more" was found to have the same effect upon the Highland regiments in Canada; and we are not sure that "Yankee Doodle," performed in the presence of a thousand Americans on the Plaza de Armas, would not secure the annexation of the island in a fortnight.

The Creoles are passionately fond of music. Their favorite airs, besides the Castilian ones, are native dances, which have much sweetness and individuality of character. They are fond of the guitar and flageolet, and are often proficients in their use, as well as possessing fine vocal powers. The voice is cultivated among the gentlemen as often as with the ladies. Music in the open air and in the evening has an invincible effect everywhere, but nowhere is its influence more deeply felt than in a starry tropical night. Nowhere can we conceive of a musical performance listened to with more delightful relish than in the Plaza at Havana, as discoursed by the governor's band, at the close of the long tropical twilight.

In the immediate neighborhood of the Plaza, near the rear of the governor's palace, is a superb confectionary,—really one of the notabilities of the city, and only excelled by Taylor's saloon, Broadway, New York. It is called La Dominica, and is the popular resort of all foreigners in Havana, and particularly of Americans and Frenchmen. It is capable of accommodating some hundreds of visitors at a time, and is generally well filled every afternoon and evening. In the centre is a large open court, paved with white marble and jasper, and containing a fountain in the middle, around which the visitors are seated. Probably no establishment in the world can supply a larger variety of preserves, bon-bons and confectionaries generally, than this, the fruits of the island supplying the material for nearly a hundred varieties of preserves, which the proprietor exports largely to Europe and America, and has thereby accumulated for himself a fortune.

Following the street on which is this famous confectionary, one is soon brought to the city walls, and, passing outside, is at once ushered into the Tacon Paseo, where all the beauty and fashion of the town resort in the after part of the day. It is a mile or more in length, beautifully laid out in wide, clean walks, with myriads of tropical flowers, trees and shrubs, whose fragrance seems to render the atmosphere almost dense. Here the ladies in their volantes, and the gentlemen mostly on foot, pass and repass each other in a sort of circular drive, gayly saluting, the ladies with a coquettish flourish of the fan, the gentlemen with a graceful wave of the hand.

In these grounds is situated the famous Tacon Theatre.

In visiting the house, you enter the first tier and parquette from the level of the Paseo, and find the interior about twice as large as any theatre in this country, and about equal in capacity to Tripler Hall, New York, or the Music Hall, Boston. It has five tiers of boxes, and a parquette with seats, each separate, like an arm-chair, for six hundred persons. The lattice-work in front of each box is light and graceful, of gilt ornament, and so open that the dresses and pretty feet of the señoras are seen to the best advantage. The decorations are costly, and the frescoes and side ornaments of the proscenium exceedingly beautiful. A magnificent cut-glass chandelier, lighted with gas, and numerous smaller ones extending from the boxes, give a brilliant light to this elegant house. At the theatre the military are always in attendance in strong force, as at all gatherings in Cuba, however unimportant, their only perceptible use, however, being to impede the passages, and stare the ladies out of countenance. The only other noted place of amusement is the Italian opera-house, within the city walls, an oven-shaped building externally, but within appropriately and elegantly furnished with every necessary appurtenance.

No object in Havana will strike the visitor with more of interest than the cathedral, situated in the Calle de Ignacio. Its towers and pillared front of defaced and moss-grown stone call back associations of centuries gone by. This cathedral, like all of the Catholic churches, is elaborately

THE CATHEDRAL AT HAVANA.

ornamented with many fine old paintings of large size and immense value. The entire dome is also decorated with paintings in fresco. The chief object of interest, however, and which will not fail to attract the attention, is a tablet of marble inlaid in the wall at the right of the altar, having upon its face the image of Christopher Columbus, and forming the entrance to the tomb where rest the ashes of this discoverer of a western world; here, too, are the iron chains with which an ungrateful sovereign once loaded him. How great the contrast presented to the mind between those chains and the reverence bestowed upon this tomb! *

The story of the great Genoese possesses a more thrilling interest than any narrative which the imagination of poet or romancer has ever conceived. The tales of the Arabian Nights, with all their wealth of fancy, are insipid and insignificant compared with the authentic narrative of the adventures of the Italian mariner and his sublime discovery. Familiar as we are with it from childhood, from the greatness of the empire he gave to Christendom, the tale has still a fascination, however often repeated, while the visible memorials of his greatness and his trials revive all our veneration for his intellect and all our interest in the story of his career. His name flashes a bright ray over the

---

* There is now being completed, at Genoa, an elaborate and most classical monument to the memory of Columbus. The work has been entrusted to a Genoese, a pupil of Canova; and, according to Prof. Silliman, who visited it in 1851, promises to be "one of the noblest of historical records ever sculptured in marble."

mental darkness of the period in which he lived, for men generally were then but just awakening from the dark sleep of the middle ages. The discovery of printing heralded the new birth of the republic of letters, and maritime en-terprise received a vigorous impulse. The shores of the Mediterranean, thoroughly explored and developed, had en-dowed the Italian states with extraordinary wealth, and built up a very respectable mercantile marine, considering the period. The Portuguese mariners were venturing far-ther and farther from the peninsula ports, and traded with different stations on the coast of Africa.

But to the *west* lay what men supposed to be an illimit-able ocean, full of mystery, peril and death. A vague con-ception that islands, hitherto unknown, might be met with afar off on that strange wilderness of waters, like oases in a desert, was entertained by some minds, but no one thought of venturing in quest of them. Columbus alone, regarded merely as a brave and intelligent seaman and pilot, con-ceived the idea that the earth was spherical, and that the East Indies, the great El Dorado of the century, might be reached by circumnavigating the globe. If we picture to ourselves the mental condition of the age, and the state of science, we shall find no difficulty in conceiving the scorn and incredulity with which the theory of Columbus was received. We shall not wonder that he was regarded as a madman or as a fool; we are not surprised to remember that he encountered repulse upon repulse, as he journeyed wearily from court to court, and pleaded in vain for aid to the sovereigns of Europe and wise men of the cloister. But the marvel is that when gate after gate was closed against him, when all ears were deaf to his patient importunities, when day by day the opposition to his views increased, when, weary and foot-sore, he was forced to beg a morsel of bread and a cup of water for his fainting and famished boy, at the door of a Spanish convent, his reason did not give way, and his great heart did not break beneath its weight of disappointment.

But his soul was then as firm and steadfast as when, launched in his frail caravel upon the ocean, he pursued day after day, and night after night, amidst a discontented, murmuring, and mutinous crew, his westward path over the trackless waters. We can conceive of his previous sorrows, but what imagination can form an adequate conception of his hopefulness and gratitude when the tokens of the neighborhood of land first greeted his senses; of his high enthusiasm when the shore was discovered; of his noble rapture when the keel of his bark grounded on the shore of San Salvador, and he planted the royal standard in the soil, the Viceroy and High Admiral of Spain in the New World! No matter what chanced thereafter, a king's favor or a king's displeasure, royal largesses or royal chains,— that moment of noble exultation was worth a long lifetime of trials. Such were our thoughts before the cathedral altar, gazing on his consecrated tomb, and thus suggestive will the visitor be sure to find this memorial of the great captain amid its sombre surroundings.*

It will be remembered that Columbus died in Valladolid, in 1506. In 1513 his remains were transferred to Seville, preparatory to their being sent, as desired in his will, to St. Domingo. When that island was ceded to France, the remains were delivered to the Spaniards. This was in 1796, one hundred and three years after they had been placed there; they were then brought with great pomp to Havana, in a national ship, and were deposited in the cathedral in the presence of all the high authorities. The church itself, aside from this prominent feature of interest, is vastly attractive from its ancient character and appearance, and one lingers with mysterious delight and thoughtfulness among its marble aisles and confessionals.

The wealth of the church and of the monks in Cuba was formerly proverbial, but of late years the major portion of the rich perquisites which they were so long permitted to receive, have been diverted in their course, so as to flow into the coffers of the crown. The priests at one time possessed large tracts of the richest soil of the island, and their revenue from these plantations was immense; but these lands were finally confiscated by the government, and, with the loss of their property, the power of the monks has also declined, and they themselves diminished in numbers. Two

---

* The reward of genius is rarely cotemporary, and even posterity is frequently most remiss in its justice. "Sebastian Cabot gave England a continent," says Bancroft, "and no one knows his burial-place!"

of their large establishments, St. Augustine and St. Domingo, have been converted into government storehouses, and the large convent of San Juan de Dios is now used solely for a hospital. Formerly the streets were thronged by monks, but now they are only occasionally seen, with their sombre dress and large shovel hats.

The character of this class of men has of former years been a scandal to the island, and the stories that are told by respectable people concerning them are really unfit for print. They led lives of the most unlimited profligacy, and they hesitated not to defy every law, moral or divine. For a long period this existed, but Tacon and subsequent governors-general, aroused to a sense of shame, made the proper representations to the home government, and put a stop to their excesses. Many persons traced the bad condition of public morals and the increase of crime just previous to Tacon's governorship directly to this ruling influence.

A fearful condition when those who assume to lead in spiritual affairs proved the fountain-head of crime upon the island, themselves the worst of criminals.

CHAPTER VII.

ONE peculiarity which is certain to strike the stranger from the first hour he lands upon the island, whether in public or private houses, in the stores or in the streets, is that the young slaves, of both sexes, under the age of eight or ten years, are permitted to go about in a state of perfect nudity; while the men of the same class, who labor in the streets, wear only a short pair of pantaloons, without any other covering to the body, thus displaying their brawny muscles at every movement. This causes rather a shock to the ideas of propriety entertained by an American; but it is thought nothing of by the "natives." On the plantations inland, the slaves of either sex wear but just enough clothes to appear decently. The almost intolerable heat when exposed to field-labor is the excuse for this, a broad palm-leaf hat being the only article that the negroes seem to desire to wear in the field.

The Calle de Mercaderes, or the street of the merchants, is the Broadway and Washington Street of Havana, and contains many fine stores for the sale of dry goods, china, jewelry, glass-ware, etc. The merchant here does not designate his store by placing his own name on his sign, but, on the contrary, adopts some fancy title, such as the " America," the " Star," the " Bomb," " Virtue," and the like ; which titles are paraded in golden letters over the doors. These tradesmen are, generally speaking, thorough Jews in their mode of dealing, and no one thinks of paying the first price asked by them for an article, as they usually make allowances for being beaten down at least one half. The ladies commonly make their purchases in the after part of the day, stopping in their volantes at the doors of the shops, from which the articles they desire to examine are brought to them by the shopmen. No lady enters a shop to make a purchase, any more than she would be found walking in the streets.

There is no paper money known on the island, so that all transactions at these stores must be consummated in specie. The coin generally in use is the Spanish and Mexican dollar, half and quarter dollars, pesétas, or twenty-cent pieces, and reals de plata, equal to our twelve-and-a-half cent pieces, or York shillings. The gold coin is the doubloon and its fractions. Silver is always scarce, and

held at a premium in Havana, say from two to five per cent.
As Cuba has no regular bank, the merchant draws on his
foreign credit altogether, each mercantile house becoming
its own sub-treasury, supplied with the largest and best of
iron safes.   The want of some legitimate banking system is
severely felt here, and is a prominent subject of complaint
with all foreign merchants.

The Spanish government supports a large army on the
island, which is under the most rigid discipline, and in a
state of considerable efficiency.   It is the policy of the
home government to fill the ranks with natives of old Spain,
in order that no undue sympathy may be felt for the Creoles,
or islanders, in case of insurrection or attempted revolution.
An order has recently been issued by Pezuela, the present
governor-general, for the enrolment of free blacks and
mulattoes in the ranks of the army, and the devotion of
these people to Spain is loudly vaunted in the captain-general's proclamation.   The enlistment of people of color in
the ranks is a deadly insult offered to the white population
of a slave-holding country,— a sort of shadowing forth of
the menace, more than once thrown out by Spain, to the
effect that if the colonists should ever attempt a revolution,
she would free and arm the blacks, and Cuba, made to
repeat the tragic tale of St. Domingo, should be useless to
the Creoles if lost to Spain.   But we think Spain overesti-
mates the loyalty of the free people of color whom she
would now enroll beneath her banner.   They cannot forget

the days of O'Donnell (governor-general), when he avenged
the opposition of certain Cubans to the illicit and infamous
slave-trade by which he was enriching himself, by charging
them with an abolition conspiracy in conjunction with the
free blacks and mulattoes, and put many of the latter to
the torture to make them confess imaginary crimes; while
others, condemned without a trial, were mowed down by the
fire of platoons. Assuredly the people of color have no
reason for attachment to the *paternal* government of Spain.
And in this connection we may also remark that this
attempt at the enrolment of the blacks has already proved,
according to the admission of Spanish authority, a partial
failure, for they cannot readily learn the drill, and officers
dislike to take command of companies.

We have remarked that the Spanish troops are in a state
of rigid discipline, and exhibit much efficiency. They are to
the eye firm and serviceable troops,— the very best, doubtless, that Spain can produce; but it must be remembered
that Spanish valor is but a feeble shadow of what it was in
the days of the Cid and the middle ages. A square of
Spanish infantry was once as impregnable as the Macedo-
nian phalanx; but they have sadly degenerated. The
actual value of the Spanish troops in Cuba may be estimated by their behavior in the Lopez invasion. They
were then called upon, not to cope with a well-appointed
and equal force, but with an irregular, undisciplined band
of less than one-fourth their number, armed with wretched

9

muskets, entirely ignorant of the simplest tactics, thrown on a strange shore, and taken by surprise. Yet nearly a full regiment of infantry, perfectly drilled and equipped, flank companies, commanded by a general who was styled the Napoleon of Cuba, were driven from the field by a few irregular volleys from their opponents. And when again the same commanding officer brought a yet greater force of every arm,— cavalry, rifles, infantry and artillery,— against the same body of insurgents, fatigued and reduced in numbers and arms, they were again disgracefully routed. What dependence can be placed upon such troops? They are only capable of overawing an unarmed population.

The Cubans seem to fear very little from the power or efforts of the Spanish troops in connection with the idea of any well-organized revolutionary attempt, and even count (as they have good reason to do) upon their abandoning the Spanish flag the moment there is a doubt of its success. They say that the troops are enlisted in Spain either by glowing pictures of the luxury and ease of a military life in Cuba, or to escape the severity of justice for the commission of some crime. They no sooner arrive in the island than the deception of the recruiting sergeants becomes glaringly apparent. They see themselves isolated completely from the people, treated with the utmost cruelty in the course of their drills, and oppressed by the weight of regulations that reduce them to the condition of machines, without any enjoyments to alleviate the wretchedness of their situation. Men thus treated are not to be relied upon in time of emergency; they can *think*, if they are not permitted to act, and will have opinions of their own.

Soldiers thus ruled naturally come to hate those in authority over them, finding no redress for their wrongs, and no sympathy for their troubles. Their immediate officers and those higher in station are equally inaccessible to them, and deaf to their complaints; and when, in the hour of danger, they are called upon to sustain the government which so cruelly oppresses them, and proclamations, abounding in Spanish hyperbole, speak of the honor and glory of the Spanish army and its attachment to the crown, they know perfectly well that these declarations and flatteries proceed from the lips of men who entertain no such sentiments in their hearts, and who only come to Cuba to oppress a people belonging to the same Spanish family as themselves. Thus the despotic system of the Spanish officers, combined with the complete isolation of the troops from the Creole population, has an effect directly contrary to that contemplated, and only creates a readiness on the part of the troops to sympathize with the people they are brought to oppress. The constant presence of a large military force increases the discontent and indignation of the Creoles. They know perfectly well its object, and regard it as a perpetual insult, a bitter, ironical commentary on the epithet of " ever faithful " with which the home government always addresses its western vassal. The loyalty of

Cuba is indeed a royal fiction. As well might a highway-
man praise the generosity of a rich traveller who surren-
ders his purse, watch and diamonds, at the muzzle of the
pistol. Cuban loyalty is evinced in an annual tribute of
some twenty-four millions of hard money; the freedom of
the gift is proved by the perpetual presence of twenty-five
to thirty thousand men, armed to the teeth ! *

The complete military force of Cuba must embrace at the
present time very nearly thirty thousand troops,— artillery,
dragoons and infantry,— nearly twenty thousand of which
force is in and about Havana. To keep such a body of
soldiers in order, when governed by the principles we have
described, the utmost rigor is necessary, and military executions are very frequent. The *garrote* is the principal
instrument of capital punishment used in the island,— a
machine contrived to choke the victim to death without
suspending him in the air. The criminal is placed in a
chair, leaning his head back upon a support prepared for it,
when a neck-yoke or collar of iron is drawn up close to the
throat. At the appointed moment, a screw is turned behind,
producing instantaneous death, the spinal cord being crushed
where it unites with the brain. This, though a repulsive

---

* " Can it be for the interest of Spain to cling to a possession that can
only be maintained by a garrison of twenty-five thousand or thirty thousand troops, a powerful naval force, and an annual expenditure, for both
arms of the service, of at least twelve million dollars ? Cuba, at this
moment, costs more to Spain than the entire naval and military establishment of the United States costs the federal government." — *Edward
Everett, on the tri-partite treaty proposition.*

idea, is far more merciful than hanging, it would seem, whereby life is destroyed by the lingering process of suffocation. The most common mode of execution, however, in the army, is the legitimate death of a soldier; and, when he is condemned, he always falls by the hands of his comrades.

The writer witnessed one of these military executions in the rear of the barracks that make the seaward side of the *Plaza de Armas*, one fine summer's morning. It was a fearful sight, and one that chilled the blood even in a tropical summer day! A Spanish soldier of the line was to be shot for some act of insubordination against the stringent army rules and regulations; and, in order that the punishment might have a salutary effect upon his regiment, the whole were drawn up to witness the scene. The immediate file of twelve men to which the prisoner had belonged when in the ranks, were supplied with muskets by their officer, and I was told that *one* musket was left without *ball*, so that each one might hope that his was not the hand to slay his former comrade, and yet a sense of mercy would cause them all to aim at the heart. The order was given; the bright morning sun shone like living fire along the polished barrels of the guns, as the fatal muzzles all ranged in point at the heart of the condemned. "*Fuego!*" (fire) said the commanding officer. A report followed, accompanied by a cloud of smoke, which the sea breeze soon dispersed, showing us the still upright form of the victim. Though wounded in many places, no vital part was touched, nor did he fall until his sergeant, advancing quickly, with a single reserved shot blew his brains over the surrounding greensward ! His body was immediately removed, the troops were formed into companies, the band struck up a lively air, and thus was a human being launched into eternity.

A very common sight in the cities or large towns of Cuba, early in the morning, is to meet a Montero from the country, riding his donkey, to the tail of which another donkey is tied, and to this second one's tail a third, and so on, up to a dozen, or less. These animals are loaded with large panniers, filled with various articles of produce; some bearing cornstalks for food for city animals; some hay, or straw; others oranges, or bananas, or cocoanuts, etc.; some with *bunches* of live fowls hanging by the feet over the donkey's back. The people live, to use a common phrase, "from hand to mouth."—that is, they lay in no stores whatever, and trust to the coming day to supply its own necessities. Hay, cornstalks, or grain, are purchased only in sufficient quantity for the day's consumption. So with meats, so with fruits, so with everything. When it is necessary to send to the market, the steward or stewardess of the house, always a negro man or woman, is freely entrusted with the required sum, and purchases according to his or her judgment and taste. The cash system is universally adopted, and all articles are regularly paid for when purchased. The Monteros, who thus bring their produce to market, wear broad palm-leaf hats, and striped shirts over brown pantaloons, with a sword by their side, and heavy spurs upon their heels. Their load once disposed of, with a strong cigar lighted in their mouths, they trot back to the country again to pile up the panniers, and on the morrow once more to supply the wants of the town. They are an industrious and manly race of yeomanry.

Few matters strike the observant stranger with a stronger sense of their peculiarity than the Cuban milk-man's mode of supplying that necessary aliment to his town or city customers. He has no cart filled with shining cans, and they in turn filled with milk (or what purports to be milk, but which is apt strongly to savor of Cochituate or Croton), so there can be no deception as to the genuine character of the article which he supplies. Driving his sober kine from door to door, he deliberately milks just the quantity required by each customer, delivers it, and drives on to the next. The patient animal becomes as conversant with the residence of her master's customers as he is himself, and stops unbidden at regular intervals before the proper houses, often followed by a pretty little calf which amuses itself by gazing at the process, while it wears a leather muzzle to prevent its interference with the supply of milk intended for another quarter. There are doubtless two good reasons for this mode of delivering milk in Havana and the large towns of Cuba. First, there can be no diluting of the article, and second, it is sure to be sweet and fresh, this latter a parti-

cular desideratum in a climate where milk without ice can
be kept only a brief period without spoiling.   Of course,
the effect upon the animal is by no means salutary, and a
Cuban cow gives but about one third as much milk as our
own. Goats are driven about and milked in the same manner.

Glass windows are scarcely known even in the cities. The
finest as well as the humblest town houses have the broad
projecting window, secured only by heavy iron bars (most
prison-like in aspect), through which, as one passes along
the narrow streets, it is nearly impossible to avoid glancing
upon domestic scenes that exhibit the female portion of the
family engaged in sewing, chatting, or some simple occupa-
tion.   Sometimes a curtain intervenes, but even this is un-
usual, the freest circulation of air being always courted in
every way.*   Once inside of the dwelling houses there are
few doors, curtains alone shutting off the communication
between chambers and private rooms, and from the corridor
upon which they invariably open.   Of course, the curtain
when down is quite sufficient to keep out persons of the
household or strangers, but the little naked negro slave
children (always petted at this age), male and female, creep
under this *ad libitum*, and the monkeys, parrots, pigeons,
and fowls generally make common store of every nook and
corner.   Doors might keep these out of your room, but

---

* " Doors and windows are all open.   The eye penetrates the whole interior of domestic life, from the flowers in the well-watered court to the
daughter's bed, with its white muslin curtains tied with rose-colored ribbons."—*Countess Merlin's Letters*.

curtains do not. One reason why the Cubans, of both sexes, possess such fine expansive chests, is doubtless the fact that their lungs thus find full and unrestrained action, living, as it were, ever in the open air. The effect of this upon the stranger is at once visible in a sense of physical exhilaration, fine spirits and good appetite. It would be scarcely possible to inhabit a house built after our close, secure style, if it were placed in the city of Havana, or even on an inland plantation of the island. The town houses are always accessible upon the roofs, where during the day the laundress takes possession, but at evening they are frequently the family resort, where the evening cigar is enjoyed, and the gossip of the day discussed, in the enjoyment of the sea breeze that sweeps in from the waters of the Gulf of Mexico.

Just outside the city walls of Havana, and on the immediate sea-coast, lies the Campo Santo, or public cemetery, not far from the city prison. It is approached by a long street of dilapidated and miserable dwellings, and is not attractive to the eye, though the immediate entrance is through cultivated shrubbery. A broad, thick wall encloses the cemetery, in which oven-like niches are prepared for the reception of the coffins, containing the better or more wealthy classes, while the poor are thrown into shallow graves, sometimes several together, not unfrequently negroes and whites, without a coffin, quicklime being freely used to promote decomposition. In short, the whole idea, and every association of the Campo Santo, is of a repulsive and disagreeable character.

This irreverent treatment of the dead, and the neglected condition of their place of sepulture, is a sad feature in a Christian country, contrasting strongly with the honors paid to the memory of the departed by semi-civilized and even savage nations. We all know the sacredness that is attached by the Turks to their burial grounds, how the mournful cypresses are taught to rise among the turbaned tombstones, and how the survivors are wont to sit upon the graves of the departed, musing for hours over the loved and lost, and seeming to hold communion with their liberated spirits. How different is it here with the Campo Santo! The bitterest pang that an Indian endures when compelled to leave his native hunting grounds, is that he must abandon the place where the ashes of his ancestors repose. The enlightened spirit which removes cemeteries from the centre of dense population is worthy of all commendation — the taste that adorns them with trees and flowers, beautifying the spot where the " last of earth " reposes, is a proof of hightoned feeling and a high civilization. Nothing of this spirit is manifested at Havana. The establishment of the cemetery without the walls of the city was a sanitary measure, dictated by obvious necessity, but there the march of improvement stopped. No effort has been made to follow the laudable example of other countries ; no, the Spanish character, arrogant and self-sufficient, will not bend to be taught by others, and will not admit a possibility of error, and they are as closely wedded to national prejudices as the Chinese. Spain is, at this moment, the most old-fashioned country of Christendom, and it is only when pressed upon by absolute necessity that she reluctantly admits of innovation.

Tacon, during his rule in the island, erected outside the city walls, and near the gate of La Punta, on the shore, a spacious prison, capable of accommodating five thousand prisoners. It is quadrangular, each side being some three hundred feet long and fifty high, enclosing a central square, planted with shrubbery and watered by a cooling and graceful fountain. The fresh breeze circulates freely through its walls, and it is considered one of the healthiest spots in the vicinity of the capital, while it certainly presents a strong contrast to the neglected precincts of the Campo Santo, hard by.

The fish-market of Havana affords probably the best variety of this article of any city in the world. The long marble counters display the most novel and tempting array that one can well imagine; every hue of the rainbow is represented, and a great variety of shapes. But a curse hangs over this species of food, plenty and fine as it is, for it is made a government monopoly, and none but its agents are permitted to sell or to catch it in the vicinity of the city. This singular law, established under Tacon, is of peculiar origin, and we cannot perhaps do better than tell the story, as gathered on the spot, for the amusement of the reader.

CHAPTER VIII.

THE STORY OF MARTI, THE SMUGGLER.

ONE of the most successful villains whose story will be written in history, is a man named Marti, as well known in Cuba as the person of the governor-general himself. Formerly he was notorious as a smuggler and half pirate on the coast of the island, being a daring and accomplished leader of reckless men. At one time he bore the title of King of the Isle of Pines, where was his principal rendezvous, and from whence he despatched his vessels, small, fleet crafts, to operate in the neighboring waters.

His story, well known in Cuba and to the home government, bears intimately upon our subject.

When Tacon landed on the island, and became governor-general, he found the revenue laws in a sad condition, as well as the internal regulations of the island; and, with a spirit of mingled justice and oppression, he determined to do something in the way of reform.* The Spanish marine sent out to regulate the maritime matters of the island, lay

---

* Tacon governed Cuba four years, from 1834 to 1838.

idly in port, the officers passing their time on shore, or in giving balls and dances on the decks of their vessels. Tacon saw that one of the first moves for him to make was to suppress the smuggling upon the coast, at all hazards; and to this end he set himself directly to work. The maritime force at his command was at once detailed upon this service, and they coasted night and day, but without the least success against the smugglers. In vain were all the vigilance and activity of Tacon and his agents — they accomplished nothing.

At last, finding that all his expeditions against them failed, partly from the adroitness and bravery of the smugglers, and partly from the want of pilots among the shoals and rocks that they frequented, a large and tempting reward was offered to any one of them who would desert from his comrades and act in this capacity in behalf of the government. At the same time, a double sum, most princely in amount, was offered for the person of one Marti, dead or alive, who was known to be the leader of the lawless rovers who thus defied the government. These rewards were freely promulgated, and posted so as to reach the ears and eyes of those whom they concerned; but even these seemed to produce no effect, and the government officers were at a loss how to proceed in the matter.

It was a dark, cloudy night in Havana, some three or four months subsequent to the issuing of these placards announcing the rewards as referred to, when two sentinels

were pacing backwards and forwards before the main
entrance to the governor's palace, just opposite the grand
plaza. A little before midnight, a man, wrapped in a cloak,
was watching them from behind the statue of Ferdinand,
near the fountain, and, after observing that the two soldiers acting as sentinels paced their brief walk so as to meet
each other, and then turn their backs as they separated,
leaving a brief moment in the interval when the eyes of
both were turned away from the entrance they were placed
to guard, seemed to calculate upon passing them unob-
served. It was an exceedingly delicate manœuvre, and
required great care and dexterity to effect it; but, at last,
it was adroitly done, and the stranger sprang lightly
through the entrance, secreting himself behind one of the
pillars in the inner court of the palace. The sentinels paced
on undisturbed.

The figure which had thus stealthily effected an entrance,
now sought the broad stairs that led to the governor's suit
of apartments, with a confidence that evinced a perfect
knowledge of the place. A second guard-post was to be
passed at the head of the stairs; but, assuming an air of
authority, the stranger offered a cold military salute and
pressed forward, as though there was not the most distant
question of his right so to do; and thus avoiding all suspicion in the guard's mind, he boldly entered the governor's reception room unchallenged, and closed the door
behind him. In a large easy chair sat the commander-in-

chief, busily engaged in writing, but alone. An expression of undisguised satisfaction passed across the weather-beaten countenance of the new comer at this state of affairs, as he coolly cast off his cloak and tossed it over his arm, and then proceeded to wipe the perspiration from his face. The governor, looking up with surprise, fixed his keen eyes upon the intruder, —

"Who enters here, unannounced, at this hour?" he asked, sternly, while he regarded the stranger earnestly.

"One who has information of value for the governor-general. You are Tacon, I suppose?"

"I am. What would you with me? or, rather, how did you pass my guard unchallenged?"

"Of that anon. Excellency, you have offered a handsome reward for information concerning the rovers of the gulf?"

"Ha! yes. What of them?" said Tacon, with undisguised interest.

"Excellency, I must speak with caution," continued the new comer; "otherwise I may condemn and sacrifice myself."

"You have naught to fear on that head. The offer of reward for evidence against the scapegraces also vouchsafes a pardon to the informant. You may speak on, without fear for yourself, even though you may be one of the very confederation itself."

"You offer a reward, also, in addition, for the discovery

of Marti, — Captain Marti, of the smugglers, — do you not ? "

" We do, and will gladly make good the promise of reward for any and all information upon the subject," replied Tacon.

" First, Excellency, do you give me your knightly word that you will grant a free pardon to *me*, if I reveal all that you require to know, even embracing the most secret hiding-places of the rovers? "

" I pledge you my word of honor," said the commander.

" No matter how heinous in the sight of the law my offences may have been, still you will pardon me, under the king's seal ? "

" I will, if you reveal truly and to any good purpose," answered Tacon, weighing in his mind the purpose of all this precaution.

" Even if I were a leader among the rovers, myself? "

The governor hesitated for a moment, canvassing in a single glance the subject before him, and then said :

" Even then, be you whom you may; if you are able and will honestly pilot our ships and reveal the secrets of Marti and his followers, you shall be rewarded as our proffer sets forth, and yourself receive a free pardon."

"Excellency, I think I know your character well enough to trust you, else I should not have ventured here."

" Speak, then ; my time is precious," was the impatient reply of Tacon.

"Then, Excellency, the man for whom you have offered the largest reward, dead or alive, is now before you!"

"And you are—"

"Marti!"

The governor-general drew back in astonishment, and cast his eyes towards a brace of pistols that lay within reach of his right hand; but it was only for a single moment, when he again assumed entire self-control, and said,

"I shall keep my promise, sir, provided you are faithful, though the laws call loudly for your punishment, and even now you are in my power. To insure your faithfulness, you must remain at present under guard." Saying which, he rang a silver bell by his side, and issued a verbal order to the attendant who answered it. Immediately after, the officer of the watch entered, and Marti was placed in confinement, with orders to render him comfortable until he was sent for. His name remained a secret with the commander; and thus the night scene closed.

On the following day, one of the men-of-war that lay idly beneath the guns of Moro Castle suddenly became the scene of the utmost activity, and, before noon, had weighed her anchor, and was standing out into the gulf stream. Marti, the smuggler, was on board, as her pilot; and faithfully did he guide the ship, on the discharge of his treacherous business, among the shoals and bays of the coast for nearly a month, revealing every secret haunt of the rovers, exposing their most valuable depots and well-selected rendezvous; and many a smuggling craft was taken and destroyed. The amount of money and property thus secured was very great; and Marti returned with the ship to claim his reward from the governor-general, who, well satisfied with the manner in which the rascal had fulfilled his agreement, and betrayed those comrades who were too faithful to be tempted to treachery themselves, summoned Marti before him.

"As you have faithfully performed your part of our agreement," said the governor-general, "I am now prepared to comply with the articles on my part. In this package you will find a free and unconditional pardon for all your past offences against the laws. And here is an order on the treasury for — "

"Excellency, excuse me. The pardon I gladly receive. As to the sum of money you propose to give to me, let me make you a proposition. Retain the money; and, in place of it, guarantee to me the right to fish in the neighborhood of the city, and declare the trade in fish contraband to all except my agents. This will richly repay me, and I will erect a public market of stone at my own expense, which shall be an ornament to the city, and which at the expiration of a specified number of years shall revert to the government, with all right and title to the fishery."

Tacon was pleased at the idea of a superb fish-market, which should eventually revert to the government, and also at the idea of saving the large sum of money covered by the promised reward. The singular proposition of the smuggler was duly considered and acceded to, and Marti was declared in legal form to possess for the future sole right to fish in the neighborhood of the city, or to sell the article in any form, and he at once assumed the rights that the order guaranteed to him. Having in his roving life learned all the best fishing-grounds, he furnished the city bountifully with the article, and reaped yearly an immense profit, until, at the close of the period for which the monopoly was granted, he was the richest man on the island. According to the agreement, the fine market and its privilege reverted to the government at the time specified, and the monopoly has ever since been rigorously enforced.

Marti, now possessed of immense wealth, looked about him, to see in what way he could most profitably invest it to insure a handsome and sure return. The idea struck him if he could obtain the monopoly of theatricals in Havana on some such conditions as he had done that of the right to fish off its shores, he could still further increase his ill-gotten wealth. He obtained the monopoly, on condition that he should erect one of the largest and finest theatres in the world, which he did, as herein described, locating the same just outside the city walls. With the conditions of the monopoly, the writer is not conversant.

Many romantic stories are told of Marti; but the one we have here related is the only one that is authenticated, and which has any bearing upon the present work.

CHAPTER IX.

THERE is a monthly lottery in Havana, with prizes amounting to one hundred and ten thousand dollars, and sometimes as high as one hundred and eighty thousand dollars, under the immediate direction and control of the authorities, and which is freely patronized by the first mercantile houses, who have their names registered for a certain number of tickets each month. The poorer classes, too, by clubbing together, become purchasers of tickets, including slaves and free negroes; and it is but a few years since, that some slaves, who had thus united and purchased a ticket, drew the first prize of sixty thousand dollars: which was honestly paid to them, and themselves liberated by the purchase of their freedom from their masters. Honestly and strictly conducted as these lotteries are, yet their very stability, and the just payment of all prizes, but makes them the more baneful and dangerous in their influence upon the populace.   Though now and then a poor man becomes rich through their means, yet thousands are impoverished in their mad zeal to purchase tickets, though it cost them their last medio.   The government thus countenances and fosters a taste for gambling, while any one acquainted at all with the Spanish character, must know that the people need no prompting in a vice to which they seem to take intuitively.

The Spaniards receive credit for being a very hospitable people, and to a certain extent this is due to them ; but the stranger soon learns to regard the extravagant manifestations which too often characterize their etiquette, as quite empty and heartless.   Let a stranger enter the house of a Cuban for the first time, and the host or hostess of the mansion says at once, either in such words or their equivalent, " All that we have is at your service; take what you will, and our right hand with it."   Yet no one thinks of understanding this literally.   The family volante is at your order, or a saddle horse ; and in such small kindnesses they are indeed polite ; but when they beg of you to accept a ring, a book, a valuable toy, because you have happened to praise it, you are by no means to do so.   Another trait of character which suggests itself in this connection, is their universal habit of profuse compliment.*   The ladies listen

---

* The common salutation, on being introduced or meeting a lady, is, " *A los pies de usted señora* " (at the feet of your grace, my lady).

to them, as a matter of course, from their countrymen, or
from such Frenchmen as have become domesticated in the
island; but if an American takes occasion to compliment
them, they are at once delighted, for they believe them to
be sincere, and the matter is secretly treasured to be
repeated.

The Cuban ladies, with true feminine acuteness, estimate
correctly the high-flown compliments of their countrymen;
and the kindred French, Castilian and Parisian politeness is
of about equal value, and means the same thing,— that is,
nothing. To strangers it is very pleasant at first, but the
moment it is apparent that these profuse protestations of
friendship and offers of service are transparent devices, and
that if you take them at their word they are embarrassed,
perhaps offended, that you must be constantly on your
guard, and be very careful to consider every fine phrase as
a flower of rhetoric, it becomes positively disagreeable.
Good manners go a great way; and if a person does you a
favor, the pleasure you experience is much enhanced by the
grace with which the obligation is conferred; but there is a
vast difference between true and false politeness. The
former springs only from a good and true heart; the latter
is especially egotistical. Both the French and Spanish are
extremely gallant to women; and yet the condition of
women in both France and Spain is vastly inferior to that
of our fair countrywomen, notwithstanding the Spanish
caballero and the Parisian *elegant* can couch their heart-

less compliments in terms our plain people would vainly attempt to imitate. But what cares a woman for fine phrases, if she knows that the respect due to her sex is wanting? The condition of the women of Cuba is emi- nently Spanish, and she is here too often the slave of pas- sion and the victim of jealousy.

The bonnet, which forms so important a part of the ladies' costume in Europe and American cities, is entirely unknown, or, rather, never worn by the Creole ladies; and strangers who appear with this article of dress are regarded with as much curiosity as we should be exercised by to meet in our own streets a Tuscarora chief in his war-paint. In place of the bonnet the Cuban ladies wear a long black veil, gathered at the back of the head upon the clustered braid of hair (always dark and luxuriant), and drawn to one side of the face or the other, as circumstances may require. More frequently, however, even this appendage is not seen, and they ride in the Paseos and streets with their heads entirely uncovered, save by the sheltering hood of the volante. When necessity calls them abroad during the early or middle hours of the day, there is a canvas screen buttoning to the dasher, and extending to the top of the vehicle, forming a partial shelter from the sun. This appa- ratus is universally arranged upon the volantes which stand at the corners of the streets for common hire; but the pri- vate vehicles are rarely seen much abroad before the early twilight, or just before sunset.

Full dress, on all state occasions, with the Cuban ladies, is black; but white is worn on all ordinary ones, forming a rich and striking contrast to the fair olive complexions of the wearers. Jewelry is worn to a great extent, and, by those who can afford it, to the amount of most fabulous sums, of course the diamond predominating; but there is a general fondness for opals, garnets and pearls, worn in bracelets more particularly, or in bands about the hair, at the top of the forehead. There is one article without which the Cuban lady would not feel at home for a single moment; it is the fan, which is a positive necessity to her, and she learns its coquettish and graceful use from very childhood. Formed of various rich materials, it glitters in her hand like a gaudy butterfly, now half, now wholly shading her radiant face, which quickly peeps out again from behind its shelter, like the moon from out a gilded cloud. This little article (always rich and expensive), perfectly indispensable in a Cuban lady's costume, in their hands seems almost to speak; she has a witching flirt with it that expresses scorn; a graceful wave of complaisance; an abrupt closing of it, that indicates vexation or anger; a gradual and cautious opening of its folds, that signifies reluctant forgiveness; in short, the language of the fan in a Cuban's hand is an adroit and expressive pantomime, that requires no foreign interpreter.

It may be owing to the prodigality of nature in respect to Flora's kingdom, which has led to no development among the people of Cuba, in the love and culture of flowers. Of course this remark is intended in a general point of view, there necessarily being exceptions to establish the rule. But it is a rare thing to see flowers under cultivation here, other than such as spring up from the over-fertile soil, un-planted and untended. In New Orleans one cannot pass out of the doors of the St. Charles Hotel, at any hour of the day, without being saluted first by the flavor of magno-lias, and then by a Creole flower-girl, with "Buy a bou-quet for a dime, sir?" But nothing of the sort is seen in Cuba; flowers are a drug. Nevertheless, I fear that people who lack an appreciation of these "illumined scriptures of the prairie," show a want of delicacy and refinement that even an humble Parisian grisette is not without. Scarcely can you pass from the coast of Cuba inland for half a league, in any direction, without your senses being regaled by the fragrance of natural flowers,— the heliotrope, honey-suckle, sweet pea, and orange blossoms predominating. The jessamine and cape rose, though less fragrant, are de-lightful to the eye, and cluster everywhere, among the hedges, groves and plantations.

There seems to be, at times, a strange narcotic influence in the atmosphere of the island, more especially inland, where the visitor is partially or wholly removed from the winds that usually blow from the gulf in the after part of the day. So potent has the writer felt this influence, that at first it was supposed to be the effect of some powerful

plant that might abound upon the plantations; but careful
inquiry satisfied him that this dreamy somnolence, this
delightful sense of ease and indolent luxuriance of feeling,
was solely attributable to the natural effect of the soft climate of Cuba. By gently yielding to this influence, one
seems to dream while waking; and while the sense of hear-
ing is diminished, that of the olfactories appears to be increased, and pleasurable odors float upon every passing
zephyr. One feels at peace with all human nature, and a
sense of voluptuous ease overspreads the body. Others
have spoken to the writer of this feeling of idle happiness,
which he has himself more than once experienced in the
delightful rural neighborhood of Alquizar. The only unpleasant realizing sense during the enjoyment of the condition referred to, is the fear that some human voice, or some
chance noise, loud and abrupt, shall arouse the waking
dreamer from a situation probably not unlike the pleasanter
effect of opium, without its unpleasant reäction.

As it regards the cost of living in the island, it may be
said to average rather high to the stranger, though it is
declared that the expense to those who permanently reside
here, either in town or country, is cheaper, all things considered, than in the United States. At the city hotels and
best boarding-houses of Havana and Matanzas, the charge
is three dollars per day, unless a special bargain is made for
a considerable period of time. Inland, at the houses of
public entertainment, the charge per diem is, of course, con-

siderably less; and the native style of living is nearly the same within or out of the city. The luscious and healthful fruits of the tropics form a large share of the provision for the table, and always appear in great variety at dessert. Good common claret wine is regularly placed before the guest without charge, it being the ordinary drink of the people. As to the mode of cooking, it seems to be very like the French, though the universal garlic, which appears to be a positive necessity to a Spanish palate, is very apt to form a disagreeable preponderance in the flavor of every dish. Fish, meat and fowl are so disguised with this article and with spices, that one is fain to resort to the bill of fare, to ascertain of what he is partaking. The vegetable soups of the city houses (but for the garlic) are excellent, many of the native vegetables possessing not only admirable flavor, and other desirable properties for the purpose, but being also glutinous, add much to the properties of a preparation answering to the character of our Julian soup. Oysters, though plentiful on the coast, are of inferior quality, and are seldom used for the table; but pickled oysters from the United States are largely used in the cities.

One of the pleasantest places of resort for enjoyment on the whole island, is probably the town of Guines, connected with Havana by a railroad (the first built upon the soil of Cuba), and but a few leagues from the capital.* This

* San Julian de los Guines contains from two to three thousand inhabitants.

locality is thought to be one of the most salubrious and appropriate for invalids, and has therefore become a general resort for this class, possessing several good public houses, and in many respects is quite Americanized with regard to comforts and the necessities of visitors from the United States. In Guines, and indeed in all Cuban towns, villages, and even small hamlets, there is a spacious cock-pit, where the inhabitants indulge in the sport of cock-fighting, — an absorbing passion with the humble, and oftentimes with the better classes. This indulgence is illustrative of their nature,— that is, the Spanish nature and blood that is in them,— a fact that is equally attested by their participation in the fearful contest of the bull-fight. It is really astonishing how fierce these birds become by training; and they always fight until one or the other dies, unless they are interfered with. The amount of money lost and won by this cruel mode of gambling is very large daily. Ladies frequently attend these exhibitions, the upper seats being reserved for them; and they may, not unfrequently, be seen entering fully into the excitement of the sport.

The cock-pit is a large or small circular building, not unlike, in external appearance, to a New England out-door hay-stack, its dimensions being governed by the populousness of the locality where it is erected. The seats are raised in a circle, around a common centre, where the birds are fought, or "pitted," upon prepared ground, covered with saw-dust or tan. The cocks, which are of a peculiar species of game birds, are subjected from chickenhood, so to speak, to a peculiar course of treatment. Their food is regularly weighed, and so many ounces of grain are laid out for each day's consumption, so that the bird is never permitted to grow fat, but is kept in "condition" at all times. The feathers are kept closely cropped in a jaunty style, and neck and head, to the length of three inches or more, are completely plucked of all feathers, and daily rubbed with *aguadiente* (island rum), until they become so calloused that they are insensible to any ordinary wound which its antagonist might inflict. Brief encounters are encouraged among them while they are young, under proper restrictions, and no fear is had of their injuring themselves, until they are old enough to have the *steel gaffs* affixed upon those which nature has given them. Then, like armed men, with swords and daggers, they attack each other, and the blood will flow at every stroke, the conflict being in no degree impeded, nor the birds affrighted, by the noisy cries, jeers, and loud challenges of the excited horde of gamblers who throng all sides of the cock-pit.*

Cuba has been justly styled the garden of the world, perpetual summer smiling upon its favored shores, and its natural wealth almost baffling the capacity of estimation. The waters which surround it, as we have already intimated, abound with a variety of fishes, whose bright colors, emu-

---

* The English game-cock is prized in Cuba only for crossing the breed, for he cannot equal the Spanish bird in agility or endurance.

11*

lating the tints of precious stones and the prismatic hues
of the rainbow, astonish the eye of the stranger. Stately
trees of various species, the most conspicuous being the
royal palm, rear their luxuriant foliage against the azure
heavens, along the sheltered bays, by the way-side, on the
swells of the haciendas, delighting the eye of the traveller,
and diversifying the ever-charming face of the tropical
landscape. Through the woods and groves flit a variety of
birds, whose dazzling colors defy the palette of the artist.
Here the loquacious parrot utters his harsh natural note;
there the red flamingo stands patiently by the shore of the
lagoon, watching in the waters, dyed by the reflection of his
plumage, for his unconscious prey. It would require a
volume to describe the vegetable, animal and mineral kingdom of Cuba. Among the most familiar birds, and those
the names of which even the casual observer is apt to learn,
are the Cuba robin, the blue-bird, the cat-bird, the Spanish
woodpecker, the gaudy-plumed parrot, the pedoreva, with
its red throat and breast and its pea-green head and body.
There is also a great variety of wild pigeons, blue, gray
and white; the English ladybird, as it is called, with a
blue head and scarlet breast, and green and white back;
the indigo-bird, the golden-winged woodpecker, the ibis, the
flamingo, and many smaller species, like the humming-bird.
Parrots settle on the sour orange trees when the fruit is
ripe, and fifty may be secured by a net at a time. The
Creoles stew and eat them as we do the pigeon; the flesh is

rather tough, and as there are plenty of fine water and marsh birds about the lagoons, which are most tender and palatable, one is at a loss to account for the taste that leads the people to eat the parrot. The brown pelican is very plenty on the sea-coast, like the gull off our own shores, and may be seen at all times sailing lazily over the sea, and occasionally dipping for fish. Here, as among other tropical regions, and even in some southern sections of this country, the lazy-looking bald-headed vulture is protected by law, being a sort of natural scavenger or remover of carrion.

The agriculturists of the island confine their attention almost solely to the raising of sugar, coffee and tobacco, almost entirely neglecting Indian corn (which the first settlers found indigenous here), and but slightly attending to the varieties of the orange.* It is scarcely creditable that, when the generous soil produces from two to three crops annually, the vegetable wealth of this island should be so poorly developed. It is capable of supporting a population of almost any density, and yet the largest estimate gives only a million and a half of inhabitants. On treading the fertile soil, and on beholding the clustering fruits offered on all sides, the delicious oranges, the perfumed pine-apples, the luscious bananas, the cooling cocoanuts, and other fruits

---

* Three years after the seed of the orange tree is deposited in the soil, the tree is twelve or fifteen feet high, and the fourth year it produces a hundred oranges. At ten years of age it bears from three to four thousand, thus proving vastly profitable.

for which our language has no name, we are struck with the
thought of how much Providence, and how little man, has
done for this Eden of the Gulf.   We long to see it peopled
by men who can appreciate the gifts of nature, men who are
willing to do their part in reward for her bounty, men who
will meet her half way and second her spontaneous efforts.*
Nowhere on the face of the globe would intelligent labor
meet with a richer reward,— nowhere on the face of the
globe would repose from labor be so sweet.   The hour of
rest here sinks upon the face of nature with a peculiar
charm; the night breeze comes with its gentle wing to fan
the weary frame, and no danger lurks in its career.   It has
free scope through the unglazed windows.   Beautifully blue
are the heavens, and festally bright the stars of a tropical
night.   Preëminent in brilliancy among the constellations
is the Southern Cross, a galaxy of stars that never greets
us in the north.   At midnight its glittering framework
stands erect; that solemn hour passed, the Cross declines.†
How glorious the night where such a heavenly sentinel indicates its watches !   Cuba is indeed a land of enchantment,
where nature is beautiful, and where mere existence is a
luxury, but it requires the infusion of a sterner, more self-

---

* "This favored land wants nothing but *men* to turn its advantages to
account, and enjoy their results, to be acknowledged as the garden of the
world." — *Alexander H. Everett.*

† Humboldt tells us that he has often heard the herdsmen in South
America say, "Midnight is past — the Southern Cross begins to
bend."

denying and enterprising race to fully test its capabilities, and to astonish the world with its productiveness.

We have thus dilated upon the natural resources of Cuba, and depicted the charms that rest about her; but every picture has its dark side, and the political situation of the island is the reverse in the present instance. Her wrongs are multifarious, and the restrictions placed upon her by her oppressors are each and all of so heinous and tyrannical a character, that a chapter upon each would be insufficient to place them in their true light before the world. There is, however, no better way of placing the grievances of the Cubans, as emanating from the home government, clearly before the reader, than by stating such of them as occur readily to the writer's mind in brief: —

She is permitted no voice in the Cortes; the press is under the vilest censorship; farmers are compelled to pay ten per cent. on all their harvest except sugar, and on that article two and a half per cent.; the island has been under martial law since 1825; over $23,000,000 of taxes are levied upon the inhabitants, to be squandered by Spain; ice is monopolized by the government; flour is so taxed as to be inadmissible; a Creole must purchase a license before he can invite a few friends to take a cup of tea at his board; there is a stamped paper, made legally necessary for special purposes of contract, costing eight dollars per sheet; no goods, either in or out of doors, can be sold without a license; the natives of the island are excluded entirely from the

army, the judiciary, the treasury, and the customs; the
military government assumes the charge of the schools;
the grazing of cattle is taxed exorbitantly; newspapers
from abroad, with few exceptions, are contraband; letters
passing through the post are opened and purged of their
contents before delivery; fishing on the coast is forbidden,
being a government monopoly; planters are forbidden to
send their sons to the United States for educational purposes; the slave-trade is secretly encouraged by government; no person can remove from one house to another
without first paying for a government permit; all cattle (the
same as goods) that are sold must pay six per cent. of their
value to government; in short, every possible subterfuge is
resorted to by the government officials to swindle the people,* everything being taxed, and there is no appeal from
the decision of the captain-general !

* " No such extent of taxation, as is now enforced in Cuba, was ever
known or heard of before in any part of the world ; and no community,
relying solely on the products of its own labor, could possibly exist
under it." — *Alexander H. Everett.*

A CUBAN VOLANTE IN THE PASEO.

CHAPTER X.

THE volante, that one vehicle of Cuba, has been several
times referred to in the foregoing pages. It is difficult without experience to form an idea of its extraordinary ease of
motion or its appropriateness to the peculiarities of the
country.* It makes nothing of the deep mud that accom-
panies the rainy season, but, with its enormous wheels, six
feet in diameter, heavy shafts, and low-hung, chaise-like
body, it dashes over and through every impediment with the
utmost facility. Strange as it may seem, it is very light
upon the horse, which is also bestridden by the postilion, or
calisero. When travelling any distance upon the road, a
second horse is added on the left, abreast, and attached to

---

* "When I first saw the rocking motion of the volante as it drove along
the streets, I thought ' that must be an extremely disagreeable carriage ! '
but when I was seated in one, I seemed to myself rocked in a cloud. I
have never felt an easier motion." — *Miss Bremer's Letters.*

the volante by an added whiffletree and traces. When there
are two horses in this style, the postilion rides the one to
the left, leaving the shaft horse free of other weight than
that of the vehicle.

When the roads are particularly bad and there is more
than usual weight to carry, of baggage, etc., a third horse
is often used, but he is still placed abreast with the others,
to the right of the shaft horse, and guided by a bridle rein
in the hands of the calisero. The Spaniards take great
pride in these volantes, especially those improved for city
use, and they are often to be met with elaborately mounted
with silver, and in many instances with gold, wrought with
great skill and beauty. There were volantes pointed out to
the writer, of this latter character, in Havana, that could
not have cost less than two thousand dollars each, and this
for a two-wheeled vehicle. A volante equipped in this
style, with the gaily dressed calisero, his scarlet jacket elaborately trimmed with silver braid, his high jack-boots with
silver buckles at the knee, and monstrous spurs upon his
heels, with rowels an inch long, makes quite a dashing appearance, especially if a couple of blackeyed Creole ladies
happen to constitute the freight. Thus they direct their
way to the Tacon Paseo, to meet the fashion of the town at
the close of the day — almost the only out-door recreation
for the sex.

Of all the games and sports of the Cubans, that of the
bull-fight is the most cruel and fearful, and without one

redeeming feature in its indulgence. The arena for the exhibitions in the neighborhood of Havana is just across the harbor at Regla, a small town, having a most worn and dilapidated appearance.* This place was formerly the haunt of pirates, upon whose depredations and boldness the government, for reasons best known to itself, shut its official eyes; more latterly it has been the hailing place for slavers, whose crafts have not yet entirely disappeared, though the rigor of the English and French cruisers in the Gulf has rendered it necessary for them to seek a less exposed rendezvous. Of the Spanish marine they entertain no fear; there is the most perfect understanding on this point, treaty stipulations touching the slave-trade, between Spain, England and France, to the contrary notwithstanding.† But we were referring to the subject of the bull-fights. The arena at Regla, for this purpose, is a large circular enclosure of sufficient dimensions to seat six thousand people, and affording perhaps a little more than half an acre of ground for the fight.

The seats are raised one above another in a circle around, at a secure height from the dangerous struggle which is sure to characterize each exhibition. On the occasion when the writer was present, after a flourish of trumpets, a large bull was let loose from a stall opening into the pit of the

* Regla now contains some seven thousand inhabitants, and is chiefly engaged in the exportation of molasses, which is here kept in large tanks.

† An intelligent letter-writer estimates the present annual importation of slaves at not less than 10,000 souls, direct from Africa.

enclosure, where three Spaniards (*toreadors*), one on foot and two on horseback, were ready to receive him, the former armed with a sword, the latter with spears. They were three hardened villains, if the human countenance can be relied upon as shadowing forth the inner man, seemingly reckless to the last degree, but very expert, agile, and wary. These men commenced at once to worry and torment the bull until they should arouse him to a state of frenzy. Short spears were thrust into his neck and sides with rockets attached, which exploded into his very flesh, burning and affrighting the poor creature. Thrusts from the horsemen's spears were made into his flesh, and while he was bleeding thus at every pore, gaudy colors were shaken before his glowing eyes; and wherever he turned to escape his tormentors, he was sure to be met with some freshly devised expedient of torment, until at last the creature became indeed perfectly infuriated and frantically mad. Now the fight was in earnest !

In vain did the bull plunge gallantly and desperately at his enemies, they were far too expert for him. They had made this game their business perhaps for years. Each rush he made upon them was easily avoided, and he passed them by, until, in his headlong course, he thrust his horns deep into the boards of the enclosure. The idea, of course, was not to give him any fatal wounds at the outset, and thus dispatch him at once, but to worry and torment him to the last. One of the gladiators now attacked him closely with the sword, and dexterously wounded him in the back of the neck at each plunge the animal made towards him, at the same time springing on one side to avoid the shock. After a long fight and at a grand flourish of trumpets, the most skilful of the swordsmen stood firm and received the infuriated beast on the point of his weapon, which was aimed at a fatal spot above the frontlet, leading direct to the brain. The effect was electrical, and like dropping the curtain upon a play : the animal staggered, reeled a moment, and fell dead ! Three bulls were thus destroyed, the last one in his frenzy goring a fine spirited horse, on which one of the gladiators was mounted, to death, and trampling his rider fearfully. During the exhibition, the parties in the arena were encouraged to feats of daring by the waving of handkerchiefs and scarfs in the hands of the fair señoras and señoritas. Indeed there is generally a young girl trained to the business, who takes a part in the arena with the matadors against the bull. The one thus engaged, on the occasion here referred to, could not have exceeded seventeen years in age.*

Whatever colonial modifications the Spanish character may have undergone in Cuba, the Creole is Castilian still in his love for the cruel sports of the arena, and there is a great similarity between the modern Spaniards and the an-

* " One of the chief features in this sport, and which attracted so many, myself among the number, was a young and beautiful girl, as lovely a creature as Heaven ever smiled upon, being one of the chief actresses in the exciting and thrilling scene." — *Rev. L. L. Allen's Lecture.*

cient Romans in this respect. As the Spanish language
more closely resembles Latin than Italian, so do the Spanish people show more of Roman blood than the natives of
Italy themselves. *Panem et circenses* (bread and cir-
cuses !) was the cry of the old Roman populace, and to
gratify their wishes millions of sesterces were lavished, and
hecatombs of human victims slain, in the splendid amphi-
theatres erected by the masters of the world in all the cities
subjected to their sway. And so *pan y toros* (bread and
bulls !) is the imperious demand of the Spaniards, to which
the government always promptly responds.

The parallel may be pursued still further : the loveliest
ladies of Rome gazed with rapture upon the dying agonies
of the gladiators who hewed each other in pieces, or the
Christians who perished in conflict with the wild beasts half
starved to give them battle ! The beauteous señoras and
señoritas of Madrid and Havana enjoy with a keen delight
the terrible spectacle of bulls speared by the *picador*,
or gallant horses ripped up and disembowelled by the
horns of their brute adversaries. It is true that the ame-
liorating spirit of Christianity is evident in the changes
which the arena has undergone ; human lives are not sacrificed wholesale in the combats ; and yet the bull-fight
is sufficiently barbarous and atrocious. It is a national
institution, and, as an indication of national character, is
well worthy of attention, however repulsive to the sensi-
tive mind. The queen of England is sometimes pres-

ent on the race-track, so also the queen of Spain occupies
the royal box at the great bull-festas of Madrid. A skilful bull-fighter is a man of mark and distinction. Montez
was regarded by the Spaniards of this generation with
nearly as much respect as Don Rodriguez de Bivar in the
days of the Moorish wars, to such a point has the vaunted
chivalry of Spain degenerated! Sometimes Spanish nobles
enter the arena, and brave peril and death for the sake of
the applause bestowed upon the successful *torero*, and
many lives are lost annually in this degrading sport.

Few professional bull-fighters reach an advanced age;
their career in the arena is almost always short, and they
cannot avoid receiving severe wounds in their dangerous
career. Pepe Illo, a famous Spanish picador, was wounded
no less than twenty-six times, and finally killed by a bull.
This man and another noted *torero*, named Romero, were
possessed of such undaunted courage, that, in order to excite
the interest of the spectators, they were accustomed to con-
front the bull with fetters upon their feet. Another famous
picador in the annals of the arena was Juan Sevilla, who
on one occasion was charged furiously by an Andalusian bull
which overthrew both horse and rider. The savage animal,
finding that the legs of his fallen antagonist were so well
protected by the iron-ribbed hide of the pantaloons the bull-
fighters wear that it was impossible to make an impression on
them, lowered his horns with the intention of striking him
in the face; but the dauntless picador, seizing one of the

12*

bull's ears in his right hand, and thrusting the fingers of
the other into his nostrils, after a horrible struggle compelled him to retire.   Then, when every one looked to see
him borne out of the ring dying, he rose to his feet, called
for a fresh horse and lance, and bounding into the saddle,
attacked the bull in the centre of the ring, and driving the
iron up to the shaft in his neck, rolled him over dead.
" O," says an enthusiastic eye-witness of this prodigious
feat, " if you had heard the *vivas*, if you had witnessed
the frantic joy, the crazy ecstasy at the display of so
much courage and good fortune, like me you would have
envied the lot of Sevilla."   Such are some of the dangers
and excitements of the bull-ring ; such is the character of
some of the scenes which the gentle ladies of Cuba have
learned, not to endure, but to welcome with delight.

To look upon these ladies, you could not possibly imagine
that there was in them sufficient hardihood to witness such
exhibitions.   They are almost universally handsome, in person rather below the height of the sex with us, but with an
erect and dignified carriage, and with forms always rounded
to a delicate fullness, displaying a tendency to *enbonpoint*
quite perfection itself in point of model.*   The hair is
always black and profuse, the complexion a light olive,
without a particle of carmine, the eyes — a match for the
hair in color — are large and beautifully expressive, with a

---

* " The waist is slender, but never compressed by corsets, so that it re-
tains all its natural proportions." — *Countess Merlin's Letters.*

most irresistible dash of languor in them.* It is really difficult to conceive of a homely woman with such eyes as you are sure to find them endowed with in Cuba. They have been justly famed also for their graceful carriage, and, indeed, it is the very poetry of motion, singular as it may seem when it is remembered that for them to walk abroad is such a rarity. It is not simply a progressive move, but the harmonious play of features, the coquettish undulation of the face, the exquisite disposition of costume, and modulation of voice, rich, liquid and sweet as the nightingale's, that engage the beholder, and lend a happy charm to the majestic grace of every attitude and every step. It is a union, a harmonious consort of all these elements, that so beautifies the carriage of the Cuban ladies.

The men are, also, generally speaking, manly and goodlooking, though much lighter, smaller and more agile, than the Americans. The lazy life that is so universally led by them tends to make them less manly in physical development than a life of activity would do. It seems to be an acknowledged principle among them never to do that for themselves that a slave can do for them,— a fact that is very plainly demonstrated by the style of the volante, where the little horse is made not only to draw after him the vehicle and its contents, but also to carry upon his back a heavy

---

† " They have plump figures, placid, unwrinkled countenances, well-developed busts, and eyes the brilliant languor of which is not the languor of illness." — *W. C. Bryant's Letters.*

negro, weighed down with jack-boots and livery, as a driver,
when a pair of reins extending from the bridle to the volante would obviate all necessity for the negro's presence at
all.   But a Creole or Spaniard would think it demeaning
to drive his own volante; the thing is never seen on the
island.   The climate, we know, induces to this sense of ease.
With abundance of leisure, and the ever-present influences
of their genial clime, where the heart's blood leaps more
swiftly to the promptings of the imagination — where the
female form earliest attains its wonted beauty and longest
holds its sway over the heart — the West Indies seem pecu-
liarly adapted for romance and love.   The consequent adventures among the people are very numerous, and not,
oftentimes, without startling interest, affording such themes
and plots as a French *feuilletonist* might revel in.   An
ungraceful woman is not to be found on the island; whether
bred in the humble cottage of the Montero, or in the luxuriant mansion of the planter or citizen, she is sure to evince
all the ease and grace of polished life.   Your heart is bound
to them at once, when on parting they give you kindly the
Spanish benediction, "Go, señor, in a good hour."

The nobility of Cuba, so called, is composed of rather
original material, to say the least of it, and forms rather
a funny "institution."   There may be some thirty gentlemen dubbed with the title of Marquis, and as many more
with that of Count, most of both classes having acquired
their wealth by the carrying on of extensive sugar planta-

tions. These are sneeringly designated by the humbler classes as " sugar noblemen," nearly all of these aristocratic gentlemen having bought their titles outright for money, not the least consideration being had by the Spanish throne as to the fitness of the individual even for this nominal honor, save a due consideration for the amount of the would-be noble's fortune. Twenty-five thousand dollars will purchase either title. And yet, the tone of Cuban society may be said to be eminently aristocratic, and, in certain circles, very exclusive. The native of old Spain does not endeavor to conceal his contempt of foreigners and the Creoles, shielding his inferiority of intelligence under a cloak of hauteur; and thus the Castilians and Creoles form two quite distinct classes in the island,— a distinction which the home government endeavor to foster and promote in every way, for obvious reasons of their own.

The sugar planter, the coffee planter, the merchant, the liberal professions and the literati (this last a meagre class in numbers), stand about in the order in which we have written them, as it regards their relative degrees or social position, but wealth has the same charm here as in every part of Christendom, and the millionaire has the entrée to all classes. The Monteros, or yeomanry of Cuba, inhabit the less-cultivated portions of the soil, venturing into the cities only to sell their surplus produce, acting as " market-men " for the cities in the immediate neighborhood of their homes. When they stir abroad they are always armed cap-a-pie with sword and pistols,* and, indeed, every one carries arms upon the inland roads of Cuba. Formerly this was a most indispensable precaution, though weapons are now rarely brought into use. The arming of the Monteros, however, has always been encouraged by the authorities, as they thus form a sort of mounted militia at all times available, and, indeed, not only the most effective, but about the only available arm of defence against negro insurrections. The Montero is rarely a slave-owner himself, but frequently is engaged on the plantations during the busy season as an extra overseer. He is generally a hard taskmaster to the slave, having an intuitive hatred for the blacks.

The Monteros † form an exceedingly important and interesting class of the population of the island. They marry very young,— the girls from thirteen to fifteen, the young men from sixteen to twenty,— and almost universally rearing large families. Their increase during the last twenty years has been great, and they seem to be fast approaching to a degree of importance that will make them, like the American farmers, the bone and sinew of the land. The

---

* " The broadsword dangles by the side of the gentleman, and holsters are inseparable from his saddle ; the simplest countryman, on his straw saddle, belts on his rude cutlass, and every man with a skin less dark than an African appears ready for encounter." — *Rev. Abiel Abbot's Letters.*

† " They are men of manly bearing, of thin make, but often of a good figure, with well-spread shoulders, which, however, have a stoop in them, contracted, I suppose, by riding always with a short stirrup." — *W. C. Bryant's Letters.*

great and glaring misfortune of their present situation, is the want of intelligence and cultivation; books they have none, nor, of course, schools. It is said that they have been somewhat aroused, of late, from this condition of lethargy concerning education, and that efforts are being made among them to a considerable extent to afford their children opportunity for instruction. Physically speaking, they are a fine yeomanry, and, if they could be rendered intelligent, would in time become what nature seems to have designed them for,— the real masters of the country.

There is one fact highly creditable to the Monteros, and that is their temperate habits, as it regards indulgence in stimulating drinks. As a beverage, they do not use ardent spirits, and seem to have no taste for the article, though at times they join the stranger in a social glass. I doubt if any visitor ever saw one of this class in the least intoxicated. This being the fact, they are a very reliable people, and can be counted upon in an emergency. As to the matter of temperance, it needs no missionaries in the island, for probably there is not so large a tract of territory in Europe or America, as this island, where such a degree of temperance is observed in the use of intoxicating drinks. Healths are drunk at table, but in sparing draughts, while delicious fruits fill up the time devoted to dessert.

There is probably but one vice that the Monteros may be said to be addicted to, or which they often indulge in, and that is one which is so natural to a Spaniard, and the appliances for which are so constantly at hand, in the shape of the cock-pit, that it is not a wonder he should be seduced by the passion of gambling. Many of the more intelligent avoid it altogether, but with others it appears to be a part and parcel of their very existence. In the cities, as we have already shown, the government encourage and patronize the spirit of gaming, as they derive from its practice, by charging exorbitant licences, etc., a heavy sum annually.

CHAPTER XI.

THE sugar plantations are the least attractive in external appearance, but the most profitable, pecuniarily, of all agricultural investments in the tropics. They spread out their extensive fields of cane without any relief whatever to the eye, save here and there the tall, majestic and glorious palm bending gracefully over the undergrowth. The income of some of the largest sugar plantations in Cuba is set down as high as two hundred thousand dollars per annum, the lowest perhaps exceeding one hundred thousand dollars. Some of them still employ ox-power for grinding the cane; but American steam-engines are fast taking the place of animal power, and more or less are monthly exported for this purpose from New York, Philadelphia and Boston. This creates a demand for engineers and machin-

13

ists, for whom the Cubans are also dependent upon this country; and there are said to be at this time two hundred Bostonians thus engaged, at a handsome remuneration, upon the island. A Spaniard or Creole would as soon attempt to fly as he would endeavor to learn how properly to run a steam-engine. As this happens to be a duty that it is not safe to entrust to even a faithful slave, he is therefore obliged to send abroad for foreign skill, and to pay for it in round numbers.

During the manufacturing season a large, well-managed sugar plantation exhibits a scene of the utmost activity and unremitting labor. The planter must "make hay while the sun shines;" and when the cane is ripe no time must be lost in expressing the juice. Where oxen are employed, they often die of over-work before the close of the season, and the slaves are allowed but five hours for sleep, though during the rest of the year the task of the negroes is comparatively light, and they may sleep ten hours if they choose.* In society, the sugar planter holds a higher rank than the coffee planter, as we have indicated in the classification already given; probably, however, merely as in the scale of wealth, for it requires nearly twice the amount of

---

* According to the Spanish slave code, the slave can be kept at work in Cuba only from sunrise till sunset, with an interval for repose at noon of two hours. But this is not regarded in the manufacturing season, which, after all, the slaves do not seem to dread, as they are granted more privileges at this period, and are better fed, with more variety of meats and spices, with other agreeable indulgences.

capital to carry on the former that is required to perfect the business of the latter, both in respect to the number of hands and also as it relates to machinery. But, as the sugar plantation surpasses the coffee in wealth, so the coffee plantation surpasses the sugar in every natural beauty and attractiveness.

A coffee plantation is one of the most beautiful gardens that can well be conceived of; in its variety and beauty baffling correct description, being one of those peculiar characteristics of the low latitudes which must be seen to be understood. An estate devoted to this purpose usually covers some three hundred acres of land, planted in regular squares of eight acres, and intersected by broad alleys of palms, mangoes, oranges, and other ornamental and beautiful tropical trees.* Mingled with these are planted lemons, pomegranates, cape jessamines, and a species of wild heliotrope, fragrant as the morning. Conceive of this beautiful arrangement, and then of the whole when in flower; the coffee, with its milk-white blossoms, so abundant that it seems as though a pure white cloud of snow had fallen there and left the rest of the vegetation fresh and green. Interspersed in these fragrant alleys is the red of the Mexican rose, the flowering pomegranate, and the large, gaudy flower of the penon, shrouding its parent stem in a cloak of scarlet, with wavings here and there of the grace-

---

* The coffee-tree requires to be protected, at least partially, from the sun ; hence the planting of bananas and other trees in their midst.

ful yellow flag, and many bewitchingly-fragrant wild
flowers, twining their tender stems about the base of these.
In short, a coffee plantation is a perfect floral El Dorado,
with every luxury (except ice) the heart could wish. The
writer's experience was mainly gained upon the estate of
Dr. Finlay, a Scotch physician long resident in Cuba, and
who is a practising physician in Havana. He has named
his plantation, in accordance with the custom of the planters, with a fancy title, and calls it pleasantly Buena Espe-
ranza (good hope).

The three great staples of production and exportation are
sugar, coffee and tobacco. The sugar-cane (*arundo sac-
charifera*) is the great source of the wealth of the island.
Its culture requires, as we have remarked elsewhere, large
capital, involving as it does a great number of hands, and
many buildings, machines, teams, etc. We are not aware
that any attempt has ever been made to refine it on the
island. The average yield of a sugar plantation affords a
profit of about fifteen per cent, on the capital invested.
Improved culture and machinery have vastly increased the
productiveness of the sugar plantations. In 1775 there
were four hundred and fifty-three mills, and the crops did
not yield quite one million three hundred thousand *arrobas*
(an arroba is twenty-five pounds). Fifty years later, a
thousand mills produced eight million arrobas; that is to
say, each mill produced six times more sugar. The Cuban
sugar has the preference in all the markets of Europe. Its

manufacture yields, besides, molasses, which forms an important article of export. A liquor, called *aguadiente*, is manufactured in large quantities from the molasses. There are several varieties of cane cultivated on the island. The Otaheitian cane is very much valued. A plantation of sugar-cane requires renewal once in about seven years. The canes are about the size of a walking-stick, are cut off near the root, and laid in piles, separated from the tops, and then conveyed in carts to the sugar-mill, where they are unladen. Women are employed to feed the mills, which is done by throwing the canes into a sloping trough, from which they pass between the mill-stones and are ground entirely dry. The motive power is supplied either by mules and oxen, or by steam. Steam machinery is more and more extensively employed, the best machines being made in the vicinity of Boston. The dry canes, after the extraction of the juice, are conveyed to a suitable place to be spread out and exposed to the action of the sun; after which they are employed as fuel in heating the huge boilers in which the cane-juice is received, after passing through the tank, where it is purified, lime-water being there employed to neutralize any free acid and separate vegetable matters. The granulation and crystallization is effected in large flat pans. After this, it is broken up or crushed, and packed in hogsheads or boxes for exportation. A plantation is renewed by laying the green canes horizontally in the ground, when new and vigorous shoots spring up from every joint, exhibiting the almost miraculous fertility of the soil of Cuba under all circumstances.

The coffee-plant (*caffea Arabica*) is less extensively cultivated on the island than formerly, being found to yield only four per cent. on the capital invested. This plant was introduced by the French into Martinique in 1727, and made its appearance in Cuba in 1769. It requires some shade, and hence the plantations are, as already described, diversified by alternate rows of bananas, and other useful and ornamental tropical shrubs and trees. The decadence of this branch of agriculture was predicted for years before it took place, the fall of prices being foreseen; but the calculations of intelligent men were disregarded, simply because they interfered with their own estimate of profits. When the crash came, many coffee raisers entirely abandoned the culture, while the wiser among them introduced improved methods and economy into their business, and were well rewarded for their foresight and good judgment. The old method of culture was very careless and defective. The plants were grown very close together, and subjected to severe pruning, while the fruit, gathered by hand, yielded a mixture of ripe and unripe berries. In the countries where the coffee-plant originated, a very different method is pursued. The Arabs plant the trees much further apart, allow them to grow to a considerable height, and gather the crop by shaking the trees, a method which secures only the ripe berries. A coffee plantation managed in this way, and combined with the culture of vegetables and fruits on the same ground, would yield, it is said, a dividend of twelve per cent. on the capital employed; but the Cuban agriculturists have not yet learned to develop the resources of their favored island.

Tobacco. This plant (*nicotiana tabacum*) is indigenous to America, but the most valuable is that raised in Cuba. Its cultivation is costly, for it requires a new soil of uncommon fertility, and a great amount of heat. It is very exhausting to the land. It does not, it is true, require much labor, nor costly machinery and implements. It is valued according to the part of the island in which it grows. That of greatest value and repute, used in the manufacture of the high cost cigars, is grown in the most westerly part of the island, known popularly as the *Vuelta de Abajo*. But the whole western portion of the island is not capable of producing tobacco of the best quality. The region of superior tobacco is comprised within a parallelo-gram of twenty-nine degrees by seven. Beyond this, up to the meridian of Havana, the tobacco is of fine color, but inferior aroma (the Countess Merlin calls this aroma the vilest of smells); and the former circumstance secures it the preference of foreigners. From Consolacion to San Christoval, the tobacco is very hot, in the language of the growers, but harsh and strong, and from San Christoval to Guanajay, with the exception of the district of Las Virtudes, the tobacco is inferior, and continues so up to Hol-

guin y Cuba, where we find a better quality. The fertile
valley of Los Guines produces poor smoking tobacco, but
an article excellent for the manufacture of snuff.   On the
banks of the Rio San Sebastian are also some lands which
yield the best tobacco in the whole island.   From this it
may be inferred how great an influence the soil produces on
the good quality of Cuban tobacco; and this circumstance
operates more strongly and directly than the slight differ-
ences of climate and position produced by immediate locali-
ties.   Perhaps a chemical analysis of the soils of the Vuelta
de Abajo would enable the intelligent cultivator to supply
to other lands in the island the ingredients wanting to
produce equally good tobacco.   The cultivators in the
Vuelta de Abajo are extremely skilful, though not scien-
tific.   The culture of tobacco yields about seven per cent.
on the capital invested, and is not considered to be so profitable on the island as of yore.

Cacao, rice, plantains, indigo, cotton, sago, yuca (a fari-
naceous plant, eaten like potatoes), Indian corn, and many
other vegetable productions, might be cultivated to a much
greater extent and with larger profit than they yield.   We
are astonished to find that with the inexhaustible fertility of
the soil, with an endless summer, that gives the laborer two
and three crops of some articles a year, agriculture generally yields a lower per centage than in our stern northern
latitudes.   The yield of a *caballeria* (thirty-two and seven-
tenths acres) is as follows:

Sugar,	.	. $2,500	Indian corn, 2 crops,		$1,500
Coffee,	.	. 750	Rice,	. .	1,000
Tobacco,	.	. 3,000	Sago,	. . .	1,500
Cacao,	. .	. 5,000	Plantains,	. .	2,500
Indigo,	.	. 2,000	Yuca,	. . .	1,000

It must be remembered that there are multitudes of fruits and vegetable productions not enumerated above, which do not enter into commerce, and which grow wild. No account is taken of them. In the hands of a thrifty population, Cuba would blossom like a rose, as it is a garden growing wild, cultivated here and there in patches, but capable of supporting in ease a population of ten times its density.

About the coffee plantations, and, indeed, throughout the rural parts of the island, there is an insect called a cucullos, answering in its nature to our fire-fly, though quadruple its size, which floats in phosphorescent clouds over the vegetation. One at first sight is apt to compare them to a shower of stars. They come in multitudes, immediately after the wet or rainy season sets in, and there is consequently great rejoicing among the slaves and children, as well as children of a larger growth. They are caught by the slaves and confined in tiny cages of wicker, giving them sufficient light for convenience in their cabins at night, and, indeed, forming all the lamps they are permitted to have. Many are brought into the city and sold by the young Creoles, a half-dozen for a paseta (twenty-five cents). Ladies not unfrequently carry a small cage of silver attached to their bracelets, containing four or five of them, and the light thus emitted is like a candle. Some ladies wear a belt of them at night, ingeniously fastened about the waist, and sometimes even a necklace, the effect thus produced being highly amusing. In the ball-rooms they are sometimes worn in the flounces of the ladies' dresses, and they seem nearly as brilliant as diamonds. Strangely enough, there is a natural hook near the head of the Cuban fire-fly, by which it can be attached to any part of the dress without any apparent injury to the insect itself; this the writer has seen apparently demonstrated, though, of course, it could not be strictly made clear. The town ladies pet these cucullos, and feed them regularly with sugar cane, of which the insects partake with infinite relish; but on the plantations, when a fresh supply is wanted, they have only to wait until the twilight deepens, and a myriad can be secured without trouble.

The Cubans have a queer, but yet excellent mode of harnessing their oxen, similar to that still in vogue among eastern countries. The yoke is placed behind the horns, at the roots, and so fastened to them with thongs that they draw, or, rather, push by them, without chafing. The animals always have a hole perforated in their nostrils, through which a rope is passed, serving as reins, and rendering them extremely tractable; the wildest and most

stubborn animals are completely subdued by this mode of
controlling them, and can be led unresisting anywhere.
This mode of harnessing seems to enable the animal to bring
more strength to bear upon the purpose for which he is
employed, than when the yoke is placed, as is the case with
us, about the throat and shoulders. It is laid down in
natural history that the greatest strength of horned animals
lies in the head and neck, but, in placing the yoke on the
breast, we get it out of reach of both head and neck, and
the animal draws the load behind by the mere force of the
weight and impetus of body, as given by the limbs.
Would n't it be worth while to break a yoke of steers to this
mode, and test the matter at the next Connecticut plough-
ing-match ? We merely suggest the thing.

The Cuban horse deserves more than a passing notice in
this connection. He is a remarkably valuable animal.
Though small and delicate of limb, he can carry a great
weight; and his gait is a sort of *march*, something
like our pacing horses, and remarkably easy under the
saddle. They have great power of endurance, are small
eaters, and very docile and easy to take care of. The
Montero inherits all the love of his Moorish ancestors
for the horse, and never stirs abroad without him. He
considers himself established for life when he possesses a
good horse, a sharp Toledo blade, and a pair of silver spurs,
and from very childhood is accustomed to the saddle.
They tell you long stories of their horses, and would make

them descended direct from the Kochlani,* if you will permit them. Their size may readily be arrived at from the fact that they rarely weigh over six hundred pounds; but they are very finely proportioned.

The visitor, as he passes inland, will frequently observe upon the fronts of the clustering dwelling-houses attempts at representations of birds and various animals, looking like anything but what they are designed to depict, the most striking characteristic being the gaudy coloring and remarkable size. Pigeons present the colossal appearance of ostriches, and dogs are exceedingly elephantine in their proportions. Especially in the suburbs of Havana may this queer fancy be observed to a great extent, where attempts are made to depict domestic scenes, and the persons of either sex engaged in appropriate occupations. If such ludicrous objects were met with anywhere else but in Cuba, they would be called caricatures, but here they are regarded with the utmost complacency, and innocently considered as ornamental.† Somehow this is a very general passion among the humbler classes, and is observable in the vicinity of Matanzas and Cardenas, as well as far inland, at

---

* "Those horses, called by the Arabians Kochlani, of whom a written genealogy has been kept for two thousand years. They are said to derive their origin from King Solomon's steeds." — *Niebuhr.*

† "On the fronts of the shops and houses, and on plastered walls by the way-side, you continually see painted birds, and beasts, and creeping things, men and women in their various vocations and amusements, and some things and some images not strictly forbidden by the letter of the commandment, being like nothing in heaven above, or in the earth beneath, or in the waters under the earth!"— *Rev. Abiel Abbot's Letters.*

the small hamlets. The exterior of the town houses is generally tinted blue, or some brown color, to protect the eyes of the inhabitants from the powerful reflection of the ever-shining sun.

One of the most petty and annoying experiences that the traveller upon the island is sure to meet with, is the arbitrary tax of time, trouble and money to which he is sure to be subjected by the petty officials of every rank in the employment of government; for, by a regular and legalized system of arbitrary taxation upon strangers, a large revenue is realized. Thus, the visitor is compelled to pay some five dollars for a landing permit, and a larger sum, say seven dollars, to get away again. If he desires to pass out of the city where he has landed, a fresh permit and passport are required, at a further expense, though you bring one from home signed by the Spanish consul of the port where you embarked, and have already been adjudged by the local authorities. Besides all this, you are watched, and your simplest movements noted down and reported daily to the captain of police, who takes the liberty of stopping and examining all your newspapers, few of which are ever permitted to be delivered to their address; and, if you are thought to be a suspicious person, your letters, like your papers, are unhesitatingly devoted to "government purposes."

An evidence of the jealous care which is exercised to prevent strangers from carrying away any information in

14

detail relative to the island, was evinced to the writer in a tangible form on one occasion in the Paseo de Isabella. A young French artist had opened his portfolio, and was sketching one of the prominent statues that grace the spot, when an officer stepped up to him, and, taking possession of his pencil and other materials, conducted him at once before some city official within the walls of Havana. Here he was informed that he could not be allowed to sketch even a tree without a permit signed by the captain-general. As this was the prominent object of the Frenchman's visit to the island, and as he was really a professional artist sketching for self-improvement, he succeeded, after a while, in convincing the authorities of these facts, and he was then, as a great favor, supplied with a permit (for which he was compelled to pay an exorbitant fee), which guaranteed to him the privilege of sketching, with certain restrictions as to fortifications, military posts, and harbor views; the same, however, to expire after ninety days from the date.

The great value and wealth of the island has been kept comparatively secret by this Japan-like watchfulness; and hence, too, the great lack of reliable information, statistical or otherwise, relating to its interests, commerce, products, population, modes and rates of taxation, etc. Jealous to the very last degree relative to the possession of Cuba, the home government has exhausted its ingenuity in devising restrictions upon its inhabitants; while, with a spirit of avarice also goaded on by necessity, it has yearly added to the burthen of taxation upon the people to an unparalleled extent. The cord *may* be severed, and the overstrained bow will spring back to its native and upright position! The Cubans are patient and long-suffering, that is sufficiently obvious to all; and yet Spain may break the camel's back by one more feather!

The policy that has suppressed all statistical information, all historical record of the island, all accounts of its current prosperity and growth, is a most short-sighted one, and as unavailing in its purpose as it would be to endeavor to keep secret the diurnal revolutions of the earth. No official public chart of the harbor of Havana has ever been issued by the Spanish government, no maps of it given by the home government as authentic; they would draw a screen over this tropical jewel, lest its dazzling brightness should tempt the cupidity of some other nation. All this effort at secrecy is little better than childishness on their part, since it is impossible, with all their precautions, to keep these matters secret. It is well known that our war department at Washington contains faithful sectional and complete drawings of every important fortification in Cuba, and even the most reliable charts and soundings of its harbors, bays and seaboard generally.

The political condition of Cuba is precisely what might be expected of a Castilian colony thus ruled, and governed by such a policy. Like the home government, she presents a remarkable instance of stand-still policy; and from one of the most powerful kingdoms, and one of the most wealthy, is now the humblest and poorest. Other nations have labored and succeeded in the race of progress, while her adherence to ancient institutions, and her dignified scorn of "modern innovations," amount in fact to a species of retrogression, which has placed her far below all her sister governments of Europe. The true Hidalgo spirit, which wraps itself up in an antique garb, and shrugs its shoulders at the advance of other countries, still rules over the beautiful realm of Ferdinand and Isabella, and its high-roads still boast their banditti and worthless gipsies, as a token of the declining power of the Castilian crown.

CHAPTER XII.

TACON'S SUMMARY MODE OF JUSTICE.

Probably of all the governors-general that have filled the post in Cuba none is better known abroad, or has left more monuments of his enterprise, than Tacon. His reputation at Havana is of a somewhat doubtful character; for, though he followed out with energy the various improvements suggested by Aranjo, yet his modes of procedure were so violent, that he was an object of terror to the people generally, rather than of gratitude. He vastly improved the appearance of the capital and its vicinity, built the new prison, rebuilt the governor's palace, constructed a military road to the neighboring forts, erected a spacious theatre and market-house (as related in connection with Marti), arranged a new public walk, and opened a vast parade ground without the city walls, thus laying the foundation of the new city which has now sprung up in this formerly desolate suburb. He suppressed the gaming-houses, and rendered the streets, formerly infested with robbers, as secure as those of Boston or New York. But all this was

14*

done with a bold military arm. Life was counted of little value, and many of the first people fell before his orders.

Throughout all his career, there seemed ever to be within him a romantic love of justice, and a desire to administer it impartially ; and some of the stories, well authenticated, illustrating this fact, are still current in Havana. One of these, as characteristic of Tacon and his rule, is given in this connection, as nearly in the words of the narrator as the writer can remember them, listened to in " La Dominica's."

During the first year of Tacon's governorship, there was a young Creole girl, named Miralda Estalez, who kept a little cigar-store in the *Calle de Mercaderes*, and whose shop was the resort of all the young men of the town who loved a choicely-made and superior cigar. Miralda was only seventeen, without mother or father living, and earned an humble though sufficient support by her industry in the manufactory we have named, and by the sales of her little store. She was a picture of ripened tropical beauty, with a finely rounded form, a lovely face, of soft, olive tint, and teeth that a Tuscarora might envy her. At times, there was a dash of languor in her dreamy eye that would have warmed an anchorite ; and then her cheerful jests were so delicate, yet free, that she had unwittingly turned the heads, not to say hearts, of half the young merchants in the *Calle de Mercaderes*. But she dispensed her favors without partiality ; none of the rich and gay exquisites of Havana could say they had ever received any particular acknowledgment from the fair young girl to their warm and constant attention. For this one she had a pleasant smile, for another a few words of pleasing gossip, and for a third a snatch of a Spanish song ; but to none did she give her confidence, except to young Pedro Mantanez, a fine-looking boatman, who plied between the Punta and Moro Castle, on the opposite side of the harbor.

Pedro was a manly and courageous young fellow, rather above his class in intelligence, appearance and associations, and pulled his oars with a strong arm and light heart, and loved the beautiful Miralda with an ardor romantic in its fidelity and truth. He was a sort of leader among the boat-men of the harbor for reason of his superior cultivation and intelligence, and his quick-witted sagacity was often turned for the benefit of his comrades. Many were the noble deeds he had done in and about the harbor since a boy, for he had followed his calling of a waterman from boyhood, as his fathers had done before him. Miralda in turn ardently loved Pedro; and, when he came at night and sat in the back part of her little shop, she had always a neat and fragrant cigar for his lips. Now and then, when she could steal away from her shop on some holiday, Pedro would hoist a tiny sail in the prow of his boat, and securing the little stern awning over Miralda's head, would steer out into the gulf, and coast along the romantic shore.

There was a famous roué, well known at this time in Havana, named Count Almonte, who had frequently visited

Miralda's shop, and conceived quite a passion for the girl,
and, indeed, he had grown to be one of her most liberal
customers.   With a cunning shrewdness and knowledge of
human nature, the count besieged the heart of his intended
victim without appearing to do so, and carried on his plan
of operations for many weeks before the innocent girl even
suspected his possessing a partiality for her, until one day
she was surprised by a present from him of so rare and
costly a nature as to lead her to suspect the donor's inten-
tions at once, and to promptly decline the offered gift.
Undismayed by this, still the count continued his profuse
patronage in a way to which Miralda could find no plausible
pretext of complaint.

    t last, seizing upon what he considered a favorable
moment, Count Almonte declared his passion to Miralda,
besought her to come and be the mistress of his broad and
rich estates at Cerito, near the city, and offered all the
promises of wealth, favor and fortune ; but in vain.   The
pure-minded girl scorned his offer, and bade him never more
to insult her by visiting her shop.   Abashed but not con-
founded, the count retired, but only to weave a new snare
whereby he could entangle her, for he was not one to be so
easily thwarted.

    One afternoon, not long after this, as the twilight was
settling over the town, a file of soldiers halted just opposite the door of the little cigar-shop, when a young man,
wearing a lieutenant's insignia, entered, and asked the

attendant if her name was Miralda Estalez, to which she
timidly responded.

"Then you will please to come with me."

"By what authority?" asked the trembling girl.

"The order of the governor-general."

"Then I must obey you," she answered; and prepared
to follow him at once.

Stepping to the door with her, the young officer directed
his men to march on; and, getting into a volante, told
Miralda they would drive to the guard-house.   But, to the
surprise of the girl, she soon after discovered that they
were rapidly passing the city gates, and immediately after
were dashing off on the road to Cerito.   Then it was that
she began to fear some trick had been played upon her; and
these fears were soon confirmed by the volante's turning
down the long alley of palms that led to the estate of Count
Almonte.   It was in vain to expostulate now; she felt that
she was in the power of the reckless nobleman, and the pre-
tended officer and soldiers were his own people, who had
adopted the disguise of the Spanish army uniform.

Count Almonte met her at the door, told her to fear no
violence, that her wishes should be respected in all things
save her personal liberty,— that he trusted, in time, to per-
suade her to look more favorably upon him, and that in all
things he was her slave.   She replied contemptuously to his
words, and charged him with the cowardly trick by which
he had gained control of her liberty.   But she was left

by herself, though watched by his orders at all times to prevent her escape.

She knew very well that the power and will of Count Almonte were too strong for any humble friend of hers to attempt to thwart; and yet she somehow felt a conscious strength in Pedro, and secretly cherished the idea that he would discover her place of confinement, and adopt some means to deliver her. The stiletto is the constant companion of the lower classes, and Miralda had been used to wear one even in her store against contingency; but she now regarded the tiny weapon with peculiar satisfaction, and slept with it in her bosom!

Small was the clue by which Pedro Mantanez discovered the trick of Count Almonte. First this was found out, then that circumstance, and these, being put together, they led to other results, until the indefatigable lover was at last fully satisfied that he had discovered her place of confinement. Disguised as a friar of the order of San Felipe, he sought Count Almonte's gates at a favorable moment, met Miralda, cheered her with fresh hopes, and retired to arrange some certain plan for her delivery. There was time to think *now ;* heretofore he had not permitted himself even an hour's sleep; but she was safe,— that is, not in immediate danger,— and he could breathe more freely. He knew not with whom to advise; he feared to speak to those above him in society, lest they might betray his purpose to the count, and his own liberty, by some means, be thus jeopardized. He could only consider with himself; he must be his own counsellor in this critical case.

At last, as if in despair, he started to his feet, one day, and exclaimed to himself, " Why not go to head-quarters at once ? why not see the governor-general, and tell him the whole truth ? Ah ! see him ?— how is that to be effected ? And then this Count Almonte is a *nobleman !* They say Tacon loves justice. We shall see. I *will* go to the governor-general ; it cannot do any harm, if it does not do any good. I can but try." And Pedro did seek the governor. True, he did not at once get audience of him,— not the first, nor the second, nor third time: but he persevered, and was admitted at last. Here he told his story in a free, manly voice, undisguisedly and open in all things, so that Tacon was pleased.

" And the girl?" asked the governor-general, over whose countenance a dark scowl had gathered. " Is she thy sister ? "

" No, Excelencia, she is dearer still; she is my betrothed."

The governor, bidding him come nearer, took a golden cross from his table, and, handing it to the boatman, as he regarded him searchingly, said,

" Swear that what you have related to me is true, as you hope for heaven ! "

" I swear ! " said Pedro, kneeling and kissing the emblem with simple reverence.

The governor turned to his table, wrote a few brief lines, and, touching a bell, summoned a page from an adjoining room, whom he ordered to send the captain of the guard to him. Prompt as were all who had any connection with the governor's household, the officer appeared at once, and received the written order, with directions to bring Count Almonte and a young girl named Miralda immediately before him. Pedro was sent to an anteroom, and the business of the day passed on as usual in the reception-hall of the governor.

Less than two hours had transpired when the count and Miralda stood before Tacon. Neither knew the nature of the business which had summoned them there. Almonte half suspected the truth, and the poor girl argued to herself that her fate could not but be improved by the interference, let its nature be what it might.

" Count Almonte, you doubtless know why I have ordered you to appear here."

" Excelencia, I fear that I have been indiscreet," was the reply.

" You adopted the uniform of the guards for your own private purposes upon this young girl, did you not ? "

" Excelencia, I cannot deny it."

" Declare, upon your honor, Count Almonte, whether she is unharmed whom you have thus kept a prisoner."

" Excelencia, she is as pure as when she entered beneath my roof," was the truthful reply.

The governor turned, and whispered something to his page, then continued his questions to the count, while he made some minutes upon paper. Pedro was now summoned to explain some matter, and, as he entered, the governor-general turned his back for one moment as if to seek for some papers upon his table, while Miralda was pressed in the boatman's arms. It was but for a moment, and the next, Pedro was bowing humbly before Tacon. A few moments more and the governor's page returned, accompanied by a monk of the church of Santa Clara, with the emblems of his office.

"Holy father," said Tacon, "you will bind the hands of this Count Almonte and Miralda Estalez together in the bonds of wedlock !"

"Excelencia !" exclaimed the count, in amazement.

"Not a word, Señor ; it is your part to obey !"

"My nobility, Excelencia !"

"Is forfeited !" said Tacon.

Count Almonte had too many evidences before his mind's eye of Tacon's mode of administering justice and of enforcing his own will to dare to rebel, and he doggedly yielded in silence. Poor Pedro, not daring to speak, was half-crazed to see the prize he had so long coveted thus about to be torn from him. In a few moments the ceremony was performed, the trembling and bewildered girl not daring to thwart the governor's orders, and the priest declared them husband and wife. The captain of the guard was summoned and despatched with some written order, and, in a few subsequent moments, Count Almonte, completely subdued and broken-spirited, was ordered to return to his plantation. Pedro and Miralda were directed to remain in an adjoining apartment to that which had been the scene of this singular procedure. Count Almonte mounted his horse, and, with a single attendant, soon passed out of the city gates. But hardly had he passed the corner of the Paseo, when a dozen musketeers fired a volley upon him, and he fell a corpse upon the road!

His body was quietly removed, and the captain of the guard, who had witnessed the act, made a minute upon his order as to the time and place, and, mounting his horse, rode to the governor's palace, entering the presence chamber just as Pedro and Miralda were once more summoned before the governor.

"Excelencia," said the officer, returning the order, "it is executed!"

"Is the count dead?"

"Excelencia, yes."

"Proclaim, in the usual manner, the marriage of Count Almonte and Miralda Estalez, and also that she is his legal widow, possessed of his titles and estates. See that a proper officer attends her to the count's estate, and enforces this decision." Then, turning to Pedro Mantanez, he said, "No man nor woman in this island is so humble but that they may claim justice of Tacon!"

The story furnishes its own moral.

CHAPTER XIII.

THE consumption of tobacco,* in the form of cigars, is absolutely enormous in the island. Every man, woman and child, seems to smoke; and it strikes one as rather peculiar, to say the least of it, to see a lady smoking her cigarito in the parlor, or on the verandah; but this is very common. The men, of all degrees, smoke, and smoke everywhere; in the houses, in the street, in the theatre, in the cafés, in the counting-room; eating, drinking, and, truly, it would seem, sleeping, they smoke, smoke, smoke. The slave and his master, the maid and her mistress, boy and man,— all, all smoke; and it is really odd that vessels don't scent Havana far out at sea before they heave in sight of its headlands.

---

* The name *tobacco* is said to have been that of the pipe used by the native Indians to inhale the smoke with, consisting of a small tube, with two branches intended to enter the nostrils.

No true Havanese ever moves a foot without his portable armory of cigars, as indispensable to him as is his quiver to the wild Indian, and he would feel equally lost without it. Some one has facetiously said that the cigar ought to be the national emblem of Cuba.

The gentlemen consume from ten to twelve cigars per day, and many of the women half that number, saying nothing of the juvenile portion of the community. The consequence of this large and increasing consumption, including the heavy export of the article, is to employ a vast number of hands in the manufacture of cigars, and the little stores and stalls where they are made are plentifully sprinkled all over the city, at every corner and along the principal streets. It is true that the ladies of the best classes in Havana have abandoned the practice of smoking, or at least they have ostensibly done so, never indulging absolutely in public; but the writer has seen a noted beauty whose teeth were much discolored by the oil which is engendered in the use of the paper cigars, thus showing that, although they no longer smoke in public, yet the walls of their boudoirs are no strangers to the fumes of tobacco. This is the only form in which the weed is commonly used here. You rarely meet a snuff-taker, and few, if any, chew tobacco. It is astonishing how passionately fond of smoking the negroes become; with heavy pipes, well filled, they inhale the rich narcotic, driving it out at the nostrils in a slow, heavy stream, and half dozing over the dreamy and exhilarating process. They are fully indulged in this taste by their masters, whether in town, or inland upon the plantations. The postilions who wait for fare in the streets pass four-fifths of their time in this way, and dream over their pipes of pure Havana.

We can have but a poor idea, at the north, of tropical fruits, for only a portion of them are of a nature to admit of exportation, and those must be gathered in an unripe condition in order to survive a short sea voyage. The orange in Boston, and the orange in Havana, are vastly different; the former has been picked green and ripened on ship-board, the latter was on the tree a few hours before you purchased it, and ripened upon its native stem. So of the bananas, one of the most delightful of all West India fruits, and which grow everywhere in Cuba with prodigal profuseness. The principal fruits of the island are the banana, mango, pomegranate, orange, pine-apple,* zapota, tamarind, citron, fig, cocoa, lemon, rose-apple and bread-fruit. Though any of these are eaten freely of at all hours, yet the orange seems to be the Creole's favorite, and he seldom rises from his bed in the morning until he has drank his cup of strong coffee, and eaten three or four oranges, brought fresh and prepared to him by a slave. The practice is one which the visitor falls very naturally into, and finds most agreeable. They have a saying that "the orange is gold in the morn-

---

* This highly-flavored and excellent fruit is so abundant in Cuba that the best sell in the market at a cent apiece.

ing, silver at noon, and lead at night." The most singular of these varieties of fruits (by no means embracing all) is the rose-apple, which, when eaten, has the peculiar and very agreeable flavor of otto of rose, and this is so strong that to eat more than one at a time is almost unpleasant. It has a very sweet taste, and flavors some soups finely. Of these fruit trees, the lemon is decidedly the most ornamental and pretty, for, though small and dwarfish, like the American quince, yet it hangs with flowers, small lemons, and ripe fruit, all together, reminding one of the eastern *Alma,** and forming an uncommon and beautiful sight. This agreeable phenomenon will surprise you at every turn upon the coffee plantations.

But the article of food most required in the island is flour, while the importation of it is made so unreasonably expensive as to amount to a positive prohibition upon the article. On foreign flour there is a fixed duty of *ten dollars,* to which if we add the one and a half per cent., with other regular charges, the duty will amount to about ten dollars and fifty cents per barrel. This enormous tax on flour prevents its use altogether in the island, except by the wealthier classes. True, there is a home-made, Spanish article, far inferior, which costs somewhat less, being imported from far-off Spain without the prohibitory clause. The estimate of the consumption of flour in this country

* "You never can cast your eyes on this tree, but you meet there either blossoms or fruit." — *Nieuhoff.*

gives one and a half barrel per head, per annum; but let us suppose that the free population consume but one. The free population — that is, the whites exclusively, not including the large number of free negroes — numbers over six hundred thousand; if the island belonged to this country, there would immediately arise a demand for six hundred thousand barrels of flour per annum, for the duty would no longer exist as a prohibition upon this necessary article. At four dollars and fifty cents per barrel, this would make the sum of two million seven hundred thousand dollars; and if we allow half a barrel each to the slaves and free blacks, which would be the natural result, being not only the best but cheapest food, we have an annual demand of from four to five hundred thousand barrels more of the great staple production of the United States. This is an item worth considering by political economists. At the present time, the imports into this country from thence exceed our exports to Cuba to the amount of nearly one million of dollars annually.

But we were writing of the vegetable productions of the island, when this digression occurred.

The Royal Palm is the noblest tree of Cuba, rising from thirty to fifty feet, and sometimes even twice this height, with a straight stem, while from the top spring the broad and beautiful leaves, in a knot, like a plume of ostrich feathers. The bark is equally divided by ornamental ringlets encircling it, each one marking a year of its age. A peculiarity of this tree is, that it has no substance in the interior of the trunk,* yet the outside, to the thickness of an inch and more, makes the finest of boards, and, when seasoned, will turn a board nail with one stroke of the hammer. The top of the palm yields a vegetable which is much 'used upon the table, and, when boiled, resembles in flavor our cauliflower. The cocoa-nut tree very much resembles the palm, the branches diverging, like the ribs of an umbrella, from one common centre, among which the fruit hangs in tempting clusters far out of reach from the ground. The plantain, with its profuse clusters of finger-like fruit, grows low like the banana, which it vastly resembles, and the entire trunk of both are renewed yearly; the old stock, after yielding its crop, decaying rapidly, and forming the most nutritious matter for the soil that can be had. Many of the hedges through the plantations are formed of aloes, of a large and luxuriant growth, with dagger-like points, and stiff, long leaves, bidding defiance to ingress or egress, yet ever ornamented with a fragrant cup-like flower. Lime hedges are also very abundant, with their clusters of white blossoms, and there is a vast supply of mahogany and other precious woods, in the extensive forests.

It is somewhat remarkable that there is not a poisonous reptile or animal of any sort in Cuba. Snakes of various

---

* It is remarkable that the palm tree, which grows so lofty, has not a root as big as a finger of the human hand. Its roots are small, thread-like, and almost innumerable.

species abound, but are said to be perfectly inoffensive, though sometimes destructive to domestic fowls. During a pleasant trip between San Antonio and Alquizar, in a volante with a planter, this subject happened to be under discussion, when the writer discovered a snake, six feet long, and as large at the middle as his arm, directly before the volante. On suddenly exclaiming, and pointing it out, the planter merely replied by giving its species, and declaring that a child might sleep with it unharmed. In the meantime, it was a relief to see the *innocent* creature hasten out of the way and secrete itself in a neighboring hedge. Lizards, tarantulas and chameleons, abound, but are considered harmless. The writer has awakened in the morning and found several lizards creeping on the walls of his apartment. Only one small quadruped is found in Cuba that is supposed to be indigenous, and that is called the hutia, much resembling a mouse, but without the tail.

The Cuban blood-hound, of which we hear so much, is not a native of the island, but belongs to an imported breed, resembling the English mastiff, though with longer nose and limbs. He is naturally a fierce, blood-thirsty animal, but the particular qualities which fit him for tracing the runaway slaves are wholly acquired by careful and expert training. This training of the hounds to fit them for following and securing the runaway negroes is generally entrusted to a class of men who go about from one plantation to another, and who are usually Monteros or French overseers out of employment. Each plantation keeps more or less of these dogs, more as a precautionary measure, however, than for actual use, for so certain is the slave that he will be instantly followed as soon as he is missed, and easily traced by the hounds, of whose instinct he is fully aware, that he rarely attempts to escape from his master. In one respect this acts as a positive advantage to the negroes themselves, for the master, feeling a confidence relative to their possession and faithfulness, and well knowing the ease with which they can at once be secured should they run away, is thus enabled to leave them comparatively free to roam about the plantation, and they undergo no surveillance except during working hours, when an overseer is of course always somewhere about, looking after them, and prompting those that are indolent.

The blood-hounds are taken when quite young, tied up securely, and a negro boy is placed to tease and annoy them, occasionally administering a slight castigation upon the animals, taking care to keep out of the reach of their teeth. This whipping is generally administered under the direction of the trainer, who takes good care that it shall not be sufficiently severe to really hurt the dogs or crush their spirit of resistance. As the dogs grow older, negro men, in place of boys, are placed to fret and irritate them, occasionally administering, as before, slight castigations upon the dogs, but under the same restrictions; and they also resort to the most ingenious modes of vexing the animals to the utmost, until the very sight of a negro will make them howl. Finally, after a slave has worried them to the last degree, he is given a good start, and the ground is marked beforehand, a tree being selected, when the dogs are let loose after him. Of course they pursue him with open jaws and the speed of the wind; but the slave climbs the tree, and is secure from the vengeance of the animals.

This is the exact position in which the master desires them to place his runaway slave — "tree him," and then set up a howl that soon brings up the hunters. They are never set upon the slaves to bite or injure them, but only placed upon their track to follow and hunt them. So perfect of scent are these animals, that the master, when he is about to pursue a runaway, will find some clothing, however slight, which the missing slave has left behind him, and giving it to the hounds to smell, can then rely upon them to follow the slave through whole plantations of his class, none of whom they will molest, but, with their noses to the ground, will lead straight to the woods, or wherever the slave has sought shelter. On the plantations these dogs are always kept chained when not in actual use, the negroes not being permitted to feed or to play with them; they are scrupulously fed by the overseer or master, and thus constitute the animal police of the plantation. In no wise can they be brought to attack a white man, and it would be difficult for such to provoke them to an expression of rage

or anger, while their early and systematic training makes
them feel a natural enmity to the blacks, which is of course
most heartily reciprocated.

Cuba has been called the hot-bed of slavery; and it is
in a certain sense true. The largest plantations own from
three to five hundred negroes, which establishments require
immense investments of capital successfully to manage. A
slave, when first landed, is worth, if sound, from four to
five hundred dollars, and more as he becomes acclimated
and instructed, their dull natures requiring a vast deal of
watchful training before they can be brought to any positive
usefulness, in doing which the overseers have found kind-
ness go a vast deal farther than roughness. Trifling rewards, repaying the first efforts at breaking in of the newly
imported negro, establishes a good understanding at once,
and thus they soon grow very tractable, though they do not
for a long time understand a single word of Spanish that
is addressed to them.

These negroes are from various African tribes, and their
characteristics are visibly marked, so that their nationality
is at once discernible, even to a casual observer. Thus the
Congos are small in stature, but agile and good laborers;
the Fantee are a larger race, revengeful, and apt to prove
uneasy; those from the Gold Coast are still more powerful,
and command higher prices, and when well treated make
excellent domestic servants. The Ebros are less black than
the others, being almost mulatto. There is a tribe known

as the Ashantees, very rare in Cuba, as they are powerful at home, and consequently are rarely conquered in battle, or taken prisoners by the shore tribes in Africa, who sell them to the slave factories on the coast. They are prized, like those from the Gold Coast, for their strength. Another tribe, known as the Carrobalees, are highly esteemed by the planters, but yet they are avoided when first imported, from the fact that they have a belief and hope, very powerful among them, that after death they will return to their native land, and therefore, actuated by a love of home, these poor exiles are prone to suicide. This superstition is also believed in by some other tribes; and when a death thus occurs, the planter, as an example to the rest, and to prevent a like occurrence among them, burns the body, and scatters the ashes to the wind!

The tattooed faces, bodies and limbs, of the larger portion of the slaves, especially those found inland upon the plantations, indicate their African birth; those born upon the island seldom mark themselves thus, and being more intelligent than their parents, from mingling with civilization, are chosen generally for city labor, becoming postilions, house-servants. draymen, laborers upon the wharves, and the like, presenting physical developments that a white man cannot but envy on beholding, and showing that for some philosophical reason the race thus transplanted improves physically, at least. They are remarkably healthy; indeed, all classes of slaves are so, except when an epidemic breaks

out among them, and then it rages more fearfully far than
with the whites. Thus the cholera and small-pox always
sweep them off by hundreds when these diseases get fairly
introduced among them. If a negro is sick he requires just
twice as much medicine as a white man to affect him, but
for what reason is a mystery in the practice of the healing
art. The prevailing illness with them is bowel complaints,
to which they are always more or less addicted, and their
food is therefore regulated to obviate this trouble as far as
possible, but they always eat freely of the fruits about them,
so ripe and inviting, and so plentiful, too, that half the crop
and more, usually rots upon the ground ungathered. The
swine are frequently let loose to help clear the ground of
its overburdened and ripened fruits.

The slaves upon the plantations in all outward circumstances seem quite thoughtless and happy; the slave code of
the island, which regulates their government, is never widely departed from. The owners are obliged to instruct them
all in the Catholic faith, and they are each baptized as soon
as they can understand the signification of the ceremony.
The law also provides that the master shall give a certain
quantity and variety of food to his slaves; but on this score
slaves rarely if ever have cause of complaint, as it is plainly
for the planter's interest to keep them in good condition.
There is one redeeming feature in Spanish slavery, as con-
trasted with that of our southern country, and that is, that
the laws favor emancipation. If a slave by his industry is

able to accumulate money enough to pay his *first cost* to his master, however unwilling the planter may be to part with him, the law guarantees him his freedom. This the industrious slave can accomplish at farthest in seven years, with the liberty and convenience which all are allowed. Each one, for instance, is permitted to keep a pig, and to cultivate a small piece of land for his own purposes, by raising corn; the land yielding two crops to the year, they can render a pig fat enough, and the drovers pay fifty dollars apiece to the slaves for good ones. This is a *redeeming* feature, but it is a bitter pill at best.

There are doubtless instances of cruelty towards the slaves, but the writer is forced to acknowledge that he never witnessed a single evidence of this during his stay in the island,* and, while he would be the last person to defend slavery as an institution, yet he is satisfied that the practical evils of its operation are vastly overrated by ignorant persons. It is so obviously for the planter's interest to treat his slaves kindly, and to have due consideration for their health and comfort — that he must be a very short-sighted being not to realize this. What man would under-feed, ill-treat, or poorly care for a horse that he expected to serve him, in return, promptly and well? We have only to consider the subject in this light for a moment, to see

---

* "I believe the lash is seldom applied ; I have never seen it, nor have I seen occasion for it." — *Rev. Abiel Abbot's Letters.*

how impossible it is that a system of despotism, severity and cruelty, would be exercised by a Cuban master towards his slaves. Let no ingenious person distort these remarks into a pro-slavery argument. God forbid !

CHAPTER XIV.

LIKE Liverpool and Boston, in their early days, Havana has drawn an immense wealth from the slave-trade; it has been the great commercial item in the business for the capital year after year, and the fitting out of ventures, the manning of vessels, and other branches of trade connected therewith, have been the sources of uncounted profit to those concerned. The vessels employed in this business were built with an eye to the utmost speed. Even before the notion of clipper ships was conceived, these crafts were built on the clipper model, more generally known as Baltimore clippers. Over these sharp hulls was spread a quantity of canvas that might have served as an outfit for a seventy-four. The consummate art displayed in their construction was really curious, and they were utterly unfit for any

16*

legitimate commerce.   Nor are these vessels by any means
yet extinct.   They hover about the island here and there
at this very hour; now lying securely in some sheltered
bay on the south side, and now seeking a rendezvous at the
neighboring Isle of Pines.   The trade still employs many
crafts.   They mount guns, have a magazine in accordance
with their tonnage, with false decks that can be shipped and
unshipped at will.

It is well known that the Americans can produce the
fastest vessels in the world; and speed is the grand desideratum with the slaver, consequently Americans are employed to build the fleet crafts that sail for the coast of
Africa.   The American builder must of course know the
purpose for which he constructs these clippers; and, indeed,
the writer is satisfied, from personal observation, that these
vessels are built on speculation, and sent to Cuba to be sold
to the highest bidder.   Of course, being in a measure contraband, they bring large prices, and the temptation is
strong to construct them, rather than to engage in the more
regular models.   This reference to the subject as connected
with the commerce of the island, leads us to look back to
the history of the pernicious traffic in human beings, from
its earliest commencement in Cuba, and to trace its beginning, progress and main features.

It has been generally supposed that Las Casas first suggested the plan of substituting African slave labor for that
of the Indians in Cuba, he having noticed that the natives,

entirely unused to labor, sunk under the hard tasks imposed upon them, while the robuster negroes thrived under the same circumstances. But negro slavery did not originate with Las Casas. Spain had been engaged in the slave trade for years, and long prior to the discovery of America by Columbus; and Zuñiga tells us that they abounded in Seville. Consequently Spanish emigrants from the old world brought their slaves with them to Cuba, and the transportation of negro slaves, born in slavery among Christians, was sanctioned expressly by royal ordinances. Ferdinand sent over fifty slaves to labor in the royal mines. Las Casas pleaded for the further employment of negroes, and consequent extension of the slave trade. " But covetousness," says Bancroft, " and not a mistaken benevolence, established the slave trade, which had nearly received its development before the charity of Las Casas was heard in defence · of the Indians. Reason, policy and religion alike condemned the traffic."

Cardinal Ximenes, the grand inquisitor of Spain, protested against the introduction of negroes in Hispaniola, foreseeing the dangers incident to their increase; and three centuries later the successful revolt of the slaves of Hayti, the first place in America which received African slaves, justified his intelligent predictions and forebodings. England embarked largely in the slave trade, and Queen Elizabeth shared in the guilty profits of the traffic. In the year 1713, when, after a period of rest, the slave trade was resumed, the English purchased of Spain a monopoly of the trade with the Spanish colonies, and she carried it on with great vigor and pecuniary success, until she had completely stocked these islands with blacks. In the year 1763 their number was estimated at sixty thousand. This fact will enable us to appreciate as it deserves the extreme modesty of the British government in fomenting abolition schemes in the island of Cuba, after contributing so largely to the creation of an evil which appears almost irremediable. We say a realizing sense of the circumstances of the case will enable us rightly to appreciate the character of the British government's philanthropy. We applaud England for her efforts at the suppression of the slave trade,— a traffic which all the powers of Christendom, Spain excepted, have united to crush,— but we cannot patiently contemplate her efforts to interfere with the internal economy of other countries, when she herself, as in the case of the Spanish colonies and of the United States, has so weighty a share of responsibility in the condition of things as they now exist; to say nothing of the social condition of her own subjects, which so imperatively demands that her charity should begin at home.

We have said that Spain alone, of the great powers, has not done her part in the suppression of the slave trade.*

* English authorities, — Sir F. Buxton in the van, — declare that the extent of the slave trade has but slightly diminished, while the restrictions under which it is now carried on renders it more fatal than ever to the blacks.

She is solemnly pledged by treaty stipulations, to make unceasing war against it, and yet she tacitly connives at its continuance, and all the world knows that slaves are monthly, almost weekly, landed in Cuba. Notorious is it that the captains-general have regularly pocketed a fee of one doubloon or more for every slave landed, and that this has been a prolific source of wealth to them. The exceptions to this have been few, and the evidences are indisputable. Within a league of the capital are several large barracoons, as they are called, where the newly-imported slaves are kept, and offered for sale in numbers. The very fact that these establishments exist so near to Havana, is a circumstance from which each one may draw his own inference. No one can travel in Cuba without meeting on the various plantations groups of the newly-imported Africans. Valdez, who strenuously enforced the treaty obligations relative to the trade, without regard to private interest, was traduced by the Spaniards, and by their management fell into disfavor with his government at home. O'Donnel deluged the island with slaves during his administration, and filled his coffers with the fees accruing therefrom. Since his time the business has gone on,— to be sure less openly, and under necessary restrictions, but nevertheless with great pecuniary profit.

At the same time the Spanish authorities have, while thus increasing the numbers of savage Africans reduced to a state of slavery, constantly endeavored to weaken the

bonds of attachment between master and slave, and to fer-
ment the unnatural hatred of races with the fearful design
of preparing another St. Domingo for the Cubans, should
they dare to strike a strenuous blow for freedom.

We have thus seen that the Spanish crown is directly
responsible for the introduction of slavery into Cuba, and
that crown officers, invested with more than vice-regal
authority, have sanctioned, up to this day, the accumula-
tion and the aggravation of the evil. It is now clearly
evident that the slave-trade will continue so long as the
island of Cuba remains under the Spanish flag. The British government have remonstrated again and again with
Spain, against this long-continued infraction of treaties;
but the dogged obstinacy of the Spanish character has been
proof against remonstrance and menace. She merits the
loss of Cuba for her persistent treachery and perfidy, leaving out of the account a long list of foul wrongs practised
upon the colony, the enormous burthen of taxes placed upon
it, and the unequalled rigor of its rule. The time has
come when the progress of civilization demands that the
island shall pass into the hands of some power possessed of
the ability and the will to crush out this remnant of barbar-
ism. That power is clearly designated by the hand of
Providence. No European nation can dream of obtaining
Cuba; no administration in this country could stand up for
one moment against the overwhelming indignation of the
people, should it be weak enough to acquiesce in the trans-

fer of Cuba to any European power. The island must be Spanish or American. Had it been the property of a first-rate power, of any other European sovereignty but Spain, it would long since have been a cause of war. It is only the imbecile weakness of Spain that has thus far protected her against the consequences of a continuous course of perfidy, tyranny and outrage. But the impunity of the feeble and the forbearance of the strong have their limits; and nations, like individuals, are amenable to the laws of retributive justice.

The present condition of Spain is a striking illustration of the mutability of fortune, from which states, no more than individuals, are exempted. We read of such changes in the destinies of ancient empires,— the decadence of Egypt, the fall of Assyria, and Babylon, and Byzantium, and Rome; but their glory and fall were both so far distant in the recess of time, that their history seems, to all of us who have not travelled and inspected the monuments which attest the truth of these events, a sort of romance: whereas, in the case of Spain, we realize its greatness, and behold its fall! One reason why we feel so deep an interest in the fate of the Castilian power, is that the history of Spain is so closely interwoven with that of our own country, — discovered and colonized as it was under the auspices of the Spanish government. We owe our very existence to Spain, and from the close of the fifteenth century our histories have run on in parallel lines. But while America has gone on increasing in the scale of destiny, in grandeur, power and wealth, poor Spain has sunk in the scale of destiny, with a rapidity of decadence no less astonishing than the speed of our own progress. The discovery of America, as before alluded to, seemed to open to Spain a boundless source of wealth and splendid power; triumphs awaited her arms in both North and South America. Cortes in Mexico and Pizarro in Peru added vast territory and millions of treasure to the national wealth. But we have seen how sure is retribution. One by one those ill-gotten possessions have escaped the grasp of the mother country; and now, in her old age, poor, and enfeebled, and worn out, she clings, with the death-gripe of a plundered and expiring miser, to her last earthly possession in the New World.

Moved in some degree by the same spirit that actuates the home government, the Cubans have heretofore viewed anything that looked like an attempt at improvement with a suspicious eye; they have learned to fear innovation; but this trait is yielding, as seen in the introduction of railroads, telegraphs, and even the lighting of the city of Havana by gas,— all done by Americans, who had first to contend with great opposition, and to run imminent risks and lavish energy and money; but when these things are once in the course of successful experiment, none are more ready than the Cubans to approve. This same characteristic, a clinging to the past and a fear of advancement, seems to have imparted itself to the very scenery of the island, for

everything here appears to be of centuries in age, reminding
one of the idea he has formed of the hallowed East. The
style of the buildings is not dissimilar to that which is
found throughout the Orient, and the trees and vegetable
products increase the resemblance. Particularly in approaching Havana from the interior, the view of the city
resembles almost precisely the Scriptural picture of Jerusa-
lem. The tall, majestic palms, with their tufted tops, the
graceful cocoanut tree, and many other peculiarities, give
to the scenery of Cuba an Eastern aspect, very impressive
to the stranger. It is impossible to describe to one who
has not visited the tropics, the bright vividness with which
each object, artificial or natural, house or tree, stands out
in the clear liquid light, where there is no haze nor smoke
to interrupt the view. Indeed, it is impossible to express
fully how *everything* differs in Cuba from our own country, so near at hand. The language, the people, the climate, the manners and customs, the architecture, the foliage, the flowers and general products, all and each afford
broad contrasts to what the American has ever seen at
home. But a long cannon-shot, as it were, off our southern
coast, yet once upon its soil, the visitor seems to have been
transported into another quarter of the globe, the first impression being, as we have said, decidedly of an Oriental
character. But little effort of the imagination would be
required to believe oneself in distant Syria, or some remote part of Asia.

But let us recur for one moment to the subject of the slaves from which we have unwittingly digressed. On the plantations the slaves have some rude ʼmusical instruments, which they manufacture themselves, and which emit a dull monotonous sound, to the cadence of which they sit by moonlight and sing or chant, for hours together. One of these instruments is a rude drum to the beating of which they perform grotesque dances, with unwearying feet, really surprising the looker-on by their power of endurance in sustaining themselves in vigorous dancing. Generally, or as is often the case, a part of Saturday of each week is granted to the slaves, when they may frequently be seen engaged at ball, playing a curious game after their own fashion. This time of holiday many prefer to pass in working upon their own allotted piece of ground and in raising favorite vegetables and fruits, or corn for the fattening of the pig hard by, and for which the drovers, who regularly visit the plantations for the purpose, will pay them in good golden doubloons. It is thought that the city slave has a less arduous task than those in the country, for he is little exposed to the sun, and is allowed many privileges, such for instance as attending church, and in this the negroes seem to take particular delight, especially if well dressed. A few gaudy ribbons, and nice glass beads of high color are vastly prized by both sexes of the slaves in town and country. In the cities some mistresses take pleasure in decking out their immediate male and female attendants in fine style with gold ornaments in profusion. There was one beautiful sight the writer particularly noticed in the church of Santa Clara, viz : that before the altar all distinction was dropped, and the negro knelt beside the Don.

The virgin soil of Cuba is so rich that a touch of the hoe prepares it for the plant, or, as Douglass Jerrold says of Australia, "just tickle her with a hoe and she laughs with a harvest." So fertile a soil is not known to exist in any other portion of the globe. It sometimes produces three crops to the year, and in ordinary seasons two may be relied upon,—the consequence is that the Monteros have little more to do than merely to gather the produce they daily carry to market, and which also forms so large a portion of their own healthful and palatable food. The profusion of its flora and the variety of its forests are unsurpassed, while the multitude of its climbing shrubs gives a luxuriant richness to its scenery, which contributes to make it one of the most fascinating countries in the world. Nowhere are the necessities of life so easily supplied, or man so delicately nurtured.

The richest soil of the island is the black, which is best adapted to the purpose of the sugar-planter, and for this purpose it is usually chosen. So productive is this description of land that the extensive sugar plantations, once fairly started, will run for years, without the soil being even turned, new cane starting up from the old roots, year after year, with abundant crops. This is a singular fact to us who

are accustomed to see so much of artificial means expended
upon the soil to enable it to bear even an ordinary crop to
the husbandman.   The red soil is less rich, and is better
adapted to the planting of coffee, being generally preferred
for this purpose, while the mulatto-colored earth is considered
inferior, but still is very productive and is improved by
the Monteros for planting tobacco, being first prepared with
a mixture of the other two descriptions of soil which together
form the richest compost, next to guano, known in agriculture.

Coal is fortunately found on the island, of a bituminous
nature ; had this not been the case, the numerous steam
engines which are now at work on the plantations would
have soon consumed every vestige of wood on the island,
though by proper economy the planter can save much by
burning the refuse cane.   The soil is also rich in mineral
wealth, particularly in copper, iron and loadstone.   Gold
and silver mines have been opened, and in former times were
worked extensively, but are now entirely abandoned.   The
copper mines near Sagua la Grande in 1841 yielded about
four millions of dollars, but the exactions of the government were such that they greatly reduced the yield of the
ore.   An export duty of five per cent. was at first imposed
upon the article : finally the exportation was prohibited altogether, unless shipped to old Spain, with a view of com-
pelling the owners to smelt it in that country.   These arbitrary measures soon reduced the profit of the business, and

the working of the mines from producing in 1841 four millions, to about two by 1845, and finally they were abandoned.

And now is it to be wondered at that the Creoles should groan under the load of oppressions forced upon them as depicted in the foregoing pages? No! On the contrary we feel that they are too forbearing, and look to the enervating influence of their clime as an excuse for their supineness under such gross wrongs. Their lovely climate and beautiful land are made gloomy by the persecutions of their oppressors; their exuberant soil groans with the burthens that are heaped upon it. They are not safe from prying inquiry at bed or board, and their every action is observed, their slightest words noted. They can sing no song not in praise of royalty, and even to hum an air wedded to republican verse is to provoke suspicion and perhaps arrest. The press is muzzled by the iron hand of power, and speaks only in adulation of a distant queen and a corrupt court. Foreign soldiers fatten upon the people, eating out their substance, and every village near the coast of the island is a garrison, every interior town is environed with bayonets!

A vast deal has been said about the impregnable harbor of Havana, the "Gibraltar of America" being its common designation, but modern military science acknowledges no place to be impregnable. A thousand chances might happen which would give the place to an invading force; besides which it has been already twice taken; and though it may be said that on these occasions it was not nearly so well garrisoned as now, neither so well armed or manned, the reply is also ready that it has never been besieged by such a force as could now be brought against it, to say nothing of the vast advantage afforded by the modern facilities for destruction.* Were not the *inaccessible* heights of Abraham scaled in a night? and how easily the impregnable fortress of San Juan de Ulloa fell! Havana could be attacked from the land side and easily taken by a resolute enemy. With the exception of this one fortress, the Moro, and the fort in its rear, the Cabensas, the island is very poorly defended, and is accessible to an invading force in almost any direction, either on the east, west, or south coast. Matanzas, but sixty miles from Havana, could be taken by a small force from the land side, and serve as a depot from whence to operate, should a systematic effort be organized. Cuba's boasted strength is chimerical.

Steam and the telegraph are revolutionizing all business relations and the course of trade. A line of steamers, one of the best in the world, runs between New York and Havana, also New Orleans and Havana. By this means all important intelligence reaches Cuba in advance of any other source, and through this country. By the telegraph, Havana is brought within three days' communication with New

* "It is as well secured as it probably could be against an attack from the harbor, but could still be assailed with effect in the same way in which the French succeeded against Algiers, by landing a sufficient force in the rear."— *Alexander H. Everett.*

York and Boston.   All important advices must continue to reach the island through the United States, and the people must still look to this country for political and commercial information, and to the movement of our markets for the regulation of their own trade and commerce.   New Orleans has become the great centre to which their interests will naturally tend; and thus we see another strong tie of common interest established between the island of Cuba and the United States.

Naturally belonging to this country by every rule that can be applied, the writer believes that Cuba will ere long be politically ours.   As the wise and good rejoice in the extension of civilization, refinement, the power of religion and high-toned morality, they will look forward hopefully to such an event.   Once a part of this great confederacy, Cuba would immediately catch the national spirit and genius of our institutions, and the old Castilian state of dormancy would give way to Yankee enterprise, her length and breadth would be made to smile like a New England landscape. Her sons and daughters would be fully awakened to a true sense of their own responsibility, intelligence would be sown broadcast, and the wealth of wisdom would shine among the cottages of the poor.

In the place of the rolling drum and piercing fife, would be heard the clink of the hammer and the merry laugh of untrammelled spirits.   The bayonets that bristle now on every hill-side would give place to waving corn, and bright

fields of grain.   The honest Montero would lay aside his
Toledo blade and pistol holsters, and the citizen who went
abroad after sun-set would go unarmed.   Modern churches,
dedicated to pure Christianity, would raise their lofty spires
and point towards heaven beside those ancient and time-
eaten cathedrals.   The barrack rooms and guard stations,
in every street, town or village, would be transformed into
school-houses, and the trade winds of the tropics would
sweep over a new Republic!

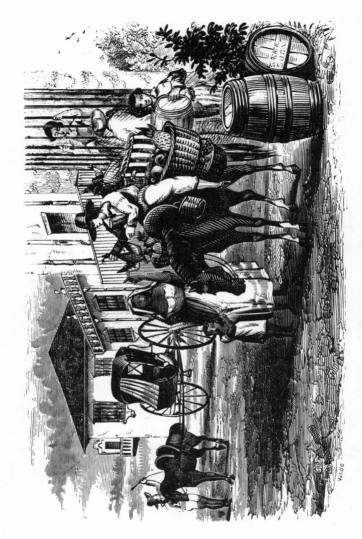

CHARACTERISTIC STREET SCENE.

CHAPTER XV.

In addition to the statistical information incidentally contained in the preceding pages, we have prepared the following tables and statements from authentic sources, giving a general view of the resources, population, wealth, products and commerce, etc., of the island, with other items of interest and importance.

Area of Cuba.— Humboldt states the area of the island to be 43,380 geographical square miles. Mr. Turnbull puts it at 31,468, and, adding the areas of its dependencies, namely, the Isle of Pines, Turignano, Romano, Guajaba, Coco, Cruz, Paredon Grande, Barril, De Puerto, Eusenachos, Frances, Largo, and other smaller islands, makes the total 32,807 square miles.

Years.						Population.
1775,	.	.	.	.	.	170,370.
1791,	.	.	.	.	.	272,140.
1817,	.	.	.	.	.	551,998.
1827,	.	.	.	.	.	704,487, viz. :

Whites, male,	.	168,653	Free colored, males,	.	51,962
" female, .	.	142,398	" females, .	.	54,532
		311,051			106,494

Slaves, 183,290 males, and 103,652 females,=286,942. Total colored, 393,436. Excess of colored over white population, 82,305.

Year 1841—

Whites,	.	.	.	.	418,291
Free colored,	.	.	.	.	152,838
Slaves,	.	.	.	.	436,495
Total,	.	.	.	.	1,007,624
Excess of colored over white,			.		171,042

Year 1851—

Whites,	.	.	.	.	605,560
Free colored,	.	.	.	.	205,570
Slaves,	.	.	.	.	442,000
Total,	.	.	.	.	1,253,130

Year 1854—

Total population, . . . 1,500,000

Proportions between the sexes.— In 1774 the white males formed 58 per cent., and the females 42 per cent., of the population; free colored, males, 52, females, 48; male slaves, 65, females, 35. Total, males, 58 per cent., females, 42.

In 1792 the proportion was —

Whites, males, ...	0.55
" females, ...	0.45
Free colored, males, . . .	0.47
" females, . . .	0.53
Slaves, males, ...	0.56
" females, ...	0.44
Total, males, ...	0.53
" females, ...	0.47

In 1817—

Whites, males, ...	0.55
" females, ...	0.45
Free colored, males, . . .	0.52
" females, . . .	0.48
Slaves, males, ...	0.62
" females, ...	0.38
Total, males, ...	0.57
" females, ...	0.53

In 1827—

Whites, males, ...	0.54
" females, ...	0.46
Free colored, males, . . .	0.48
" females, . . .	0.52
Slaves, males, ...	0.64

Slaves, females,	.	.	.	.	0.36
Total, males,	.	.	.	.	0.56
" females,	.	.	.	.	0.44

In Paris, the ratio is 54.5 per cent. males, to 45.5 females; in England, 50.3 per cent. males, and 49.7 per cent. females, and in the United States, 51 per cent. males, and 49 per cent. females.

The ratio of legitimate to illegitimate births, deduced from the observations of five years, is as follows:

2.1136 to 1 among the whites;

0.5058 to 1 among the colored;

1.0216 to 1 in the total.

That is to say, establishing the comparison per centum, as in the proportion of the sexes, we have:

Whites,	. .	67.8 per cent. legitimate, and 32.2 per cent. illegitimate.
Colored,	. .	33.7 " " " 66.3 " "
Total,	. . .	50.5 " " " 49.5 " "

No capital or people of Europe, Stockholm alone excepted, offers so startling a result, nearly one half the number of births being illegitimate.

Taking the average from the statements of births for five years, we find that in every 100 legitimate whites there are 51.1 males, and 48.9 females; and in an equal number of illegitimate, 49 males, and 51 females. Among people of color, in 100 legitimate births, 50.6 males, and 49.4 females; and in the illegitimate, 47.2 males, and 52.8 females. And finally, that, comparing the totals, we obtain in the legitimate, 51.6 males, and 48.4 females; and in the illegitimate, 47.1 males, and 52.9 females. Consequently these observations show that in Cuba, in the illegitimate births, the number of males is much less than that of females, and the contrary in the legitimate births.

Ratio between the Births and Deaths for five years.

	1825	1826	1827	1828	1829
Births, ...	3,129	3,443	3,491	3,705	3,639
Deaths, ...	2,698	2,781	3,077	3,320	3,712
Difference, . . .	431	662	414	385	73

Agriculture.— The total number of acres comprising the whole territory is 14,993,024. Of these, in 1830, there were used

In sugar-cane plantations, .	.	172,608
" coffee trees,	. . .	184,352
" tobacco,	. . .	54,448
" lesser or garden and fruit culture,		823,424
Total acres,	. . .	1,234,832

Leaving over 13,000,000 of acres uncultivated. Some of these uncultivated lands are appropriated to grazing, others to settlements and towns; the remainder occupied by mountains, roads, coasts, rivers and lakes,— the greater part, however, wild.

Total value of lands in 1830,   .   . $94,396,300

Value of buildings, utensils, etc.,   .   55,603,850

The different products of cultivation were valued as follows:

18

Sugar canes in the ground, . . .	$6,068,877
Coffee trees, ...	32,500,000
Fruit trees, vegetables, etc., . .	46,940,700
Tobacco plants, ...	340,620
Total value of plants, . . .	85,850,197

Total value of wood exported, consumed on the island and made into charcoal, .	$3,818,493
Minimum value of the forests, . .	190,624,000
Value of 138,982 slaves, at $300 each, .	41,694,600
Total value of live stock, . . .	39,617,885

RECAPITULATION.

Lands, ...	$94,396,300
Plants, including timber, . . .	276,774,367
Buildings, engines and utensils, .	54,603,850
Slaves, ...	41,694,600
Animals, ...	39,617,885
	507,087,002

Representative value of capital invested,	317,264,832

VALUE OF AGRICULTURAL PRODUCTS.

Sugar, ...	$8,132,609
Molasses, ...	262,932
Coffee, ...	4,325,292
Cocoa, ...	74,890 -
Carried forward, . . .	12,795,723

Brought forward, . . .	$12,795,723
Cotton, ...	125,000
Leaf tobacco, ...	687,240
Rice, ...	454,230
Beans, peas, onions, etc., . . .	257,260
Indian corn, ...	4,853,418
Vegetables and fruits, . . .	11,475,712
Grapes, ...	5,586,616
Casada, ...	146,144
Charcoal, ...	2,107,300
Woods or the products of woods, .	1,741,195
Total value of vegetable productions, .	40,229,838
Total value of animal productions, .	9,023,116
	49,252,954
Total *net* product of agricultural and rural industry, ...	22,808,622
Capital invested, $338,917,705, produces,	48,839,928

COMMERCE AND COMMERCIAL REGULATIONS.

Import duties.— The rate of duty charged on the importation of foreign produce and manufactures in foreign bottoms is 24½ and 30¼ on the tariff valuation of each article, while the same articles in Spanish bottoms, from a foreign port, pay 17½ and 21¼ per cent.

Export duties.— Foreign flag for any port, 6¼ per cent. on tariff valuation.

Spanish flag for a foreign port, $4\frac{1}{2}$ per cent. on tariff valuation.

Spanish flag for Spanish port, $2\frac{1}{4}$ per cent. on tariff valuation; except leaf tobacco, which pays $12\frac{1}{2}$, $6\frac{1}{4}$ and $2\frac{1}{4}$ per cent., according to the flag and destination.

An additional per centage, under various pretexts, is also levied on the total amount of all duties.

Foreign flour is subject to a duty that is nearly prohibitory.

Gold and silver are free of import duty, but pay, the former $1\frac{1}{4}$ and the latter $2\frac{1}{4}$ per cent., export.

Every master of a vessel, on entering port, is obliged to present two manifests of his cargo and stores,— one to the boarding officers, and the other at the time of making entry and taking both the oaths, twenty-four hours after his arrival, with permission of making any necessary corrections within the twelve working hours; and every consignee is required to deliver a detailed invoice of each cargo to his, her or their consignment, within forty-eight hours after the vessel has entered port, and heavy penalties are incurred from mere omission or inaccuracy.

The tonnage duty on foreign vessels is 12 rials, or \$1.50, per register ton.

On vessels arriving and departing in ballast or putting in in distress no duty is levied.

Besides the tonnage duty, every foreign square-rigged

vessel entering and loading incurs about $85 expenses, besides $5.50 for each day occupied in discharging. Foreign fore-and-aft vessels pay about $15 less port charges.

The tonnage duties and port charges are very high. Foreign vessels pay $8.50 per ton. In the port of Havana an additional duty of $21\frac{7}{8}$ cents per ton is levied on all vessels for the support of the dredging machine.

The wharf charges on foreign vessels are $1.50 for each 100 tons register.

The light-house duties, officers' fees, etc., vary at the different ports of the island, but are exorbitantly high in all. At Baracoa, for instance, the following is the tariff of exactions:

Tonnage duty, per ton, ...	$1.50
Anchorage, ...	12.00
Free pass at the fort, ...	3.00
Health officer, ...	8.00
Interpreter, ...	5.00
Inspector's fee for sealing hatchway, . .	5.00
Inspecting vessel's register, . . .	8.00
Clearance, ...	8.00

The actual expenses of discharging a foreign vessel of $160\frac{4}{9.5}$ tons, which remained a fortnight in the port of Havana, amounted to $900.

18*

IMPORTS AND EXPORTS OF CUBA FOR A SERIES OF SIX-
TEEN YEARS.

Years.	Imports.	Exports.
1826	$14,925,754	$13,809,838
1827	17,352,854	14,286,192
1828	19,534,922	13,114,362
1829	18,695,856	13,952,405
1830	16,171,562	15,870,968
1831	15,548,791	12,918,711
1832	15,198,465	13,595,017
1834	18,511,132	13,996,100
1835	18,563,300	14,487,955
1836	20,722,072	14,059,246
1837	22,551,969	15,398,245
1838	22,940,357	20,346,407
1839	24,729,878	20,471,102
1840	25,217,796	21,481,848
1841	24,700,189	25,941,783
1842	24,637,527	26,684,701

During the last year (1842), the imports from the United States were,

In Spanish vessels, ... $474,262

In Foreign do., ... $5,725,959

Exports to the United States for the same year,

In Spanish vessels, ... $243,683

In Foreign do., ... $5,038,891

Total imports from the United States, $6,200,219

  " exports to   do., $5,282,574

Total number of arrivals in Spanish ports (1842),   2657

        "   clearances from do.,   2727

The following table exhibits the exports from the principal towns in 1848 :

North Side of the Island.

	Havana.	Matanzas.	Cardenas.	Sagua la Grande.
Sugar (boxes)	671,440	318,931	13,900	34,628
Coffee (arrobas, 25lbs. each)	93,797	61,251	1,094	
Molasses (hhds.)	25,886	61,793	60,508	8,327
Rum (pipes)	10,479			1
Cigars (thousands)	136,980			62

	Mariel.	Gibaro.	Remedios.	Neuvitas.	Baracoa.
Sugar (boxes)		1,648	5,595	4,298	
Coffee (arrobas)		16,241			114
Molasses (hhds.)	8,336	16,201	1,880	5,030	
Rum (pipes)				223	
Cigars (boxes, 1000 each)		588	88	2,061	247
Tobacco (lbs.)		1,867,736		2,267	102,168

South Side.

	Manzanilla.	Trinidad.	St. Jago de Cuba.	Cienfuegos.	Santa Cruz.
Sugar (boxes)	115	69,656	31,298	59,215	198
Coffee (arrobas)		3,609	548,432	128	
Molasses (hhds.)	1,475	26,175	857	14,160	997
Rum (pipes)		60	554	379	181
Tobacco (lbs.)	315,570		1,208,536	5,000	2,669
Cigars (thousands)	542	399	4,575	41	155
Copper ore (lbs.)			571,826		

Universities, Schools, etc.— Besides the Royal University at Havana, there are several other learned institutes, such as the Royal Seminary of San Carlos y San Ambrosio, founded in 1773; a seminary for girls, founded in 1691; a free school for sculpture and painting, which dates from 1818; a free mercantile school, and some private seminaries, to which we have before referred. The Royal Economical Society of Havana, formerly called the Patriotic Society, was established in 1793, and is divided into three principal sections, on education, agriculture, commerce and popular industry; a department of history has been added. Several eminent and talented men have given eclat to this institution.

The Medical School was organized in 1842.

The means of general education are very narrow and inadequate. No report on the state of education in the island has been published since 1836. At that time, there were two hundred and ten schools for white, and thirty-one for colored children. In 1842, the public funds for educational purposes were reduced from thirty-two thousand to eight thousand dollars. Nueva Filipina, in a rich tobacco-growing district, with a population of thirty thousand souls, had but one school for forty pupils, a few years since.

Charitable Institutions, Hospitals, etc. — There are several charitable institutions in Havana. with ample funds and well managed. Such are the Casa Real de Beneficencia, the Hospital of San Lazaro and the Foundling Hospital, — Casa Real de Maternidad. In other parts of the island, there are eighteen hospitals, located in its chief towns.

Rail-roads. — The first railroad built in Cuba was that from Havana to Guines, forty-five miles in length, completed and opened in 1839.　In 1848, there were two hundred and eighty-five miles of railroads on the island, and the capital invested in them has been computed at between five and six millions of dollars.

Climate.— The diversity of surface gives rise to considerable variation in temperature.　On the highest mountain ridges, at four thousand feet above the level of the sea, ice is sometimes formed in mid winter, but snow is unknown.

The mean temperature of the hottest months (July and August) is about 83° Fahrenheit.　The coldest months are January and December.

CHAPTER XVI.

IT is with infinite reluctance that the temporary sojourner in Cuba leaves her delicious shores, and takes his farewell look at their enchanting features. A brief residence in the island passes like a midsummer - night's dream, and it requires a strenuous effort of the mind to arrive at the conviction that the memories one brings away with him are not delusive sports of the imagination. Smiling skies and smiling waters, groves of palm and orange, the bloom of the heliotrope, the jessamine, and the rose, flights of strange and gaudy birds, tropic nights at once luxurious and calm, clouds of fire-flies floating like unsphered stars on the night breeze, graceful figures of dark-eyed señoritas in diaphanous drapery, picturesque groups of Monteros, relieved by the dusky faces and stalwart forms of the sons of Africa, undulating volantes, military pageants, ecclesiastical processions, frowning fortresses, grim batteries, white sails, fountains raining silver,— all these images mingle together in brilliant and kaleidoscopic combinations, changing and varying as the mind's eye seeks to fix their features.   Long after his departure from the enchanting island the traveller beholds these visions in the still watches of the night, and again he listens to the dash of the sea-green waves at the foot of the Moro and the Punta, the roll of the drum and the crash of arms upon the ramparts, and the thrilling strains of music from the military band in the Plaza de Armas.   The vexations incident to all travel, and meted out in no stinted measure to the visitor at Cuba, are amply repaid by the spectacles it presents.

> " —— It is a goodly sight to see
> What Heaven hath done for this delicious land !
> What fruits of fragrance blush on every tree !
> What goodly prospects o'er the hills expand ! "

If it were possible to contemplate only the beauties that nature has so prodigally lavished on this Eden of the Gulf, shutting out all that man has done and is still doing to mar the blessings of Heaven, then a visit to or residence in Cuba would present a succession of unalloyed pleasures equal to a poet's dream. But it is impossible, even if it would be desirable, to exclude the dark side of the picture.   The American traveller, particularly, keenly alive to the social and political aspects of life, appreciates in full force the evils that chal-

lenge his observation at every step, and in every view which
he may take.   If he contrast the natural scenery with the familiar pictures of home, he cannot help also contrasting the
political condition of the people with that of his own country.
The existence, almost under the shadow of the flag of the
freest institutions the earth ever knew, of a government as
purely despotic as that of the autocrat of all the Russias,
is a monstrous fact that startles the most indifferent observer.   It must be seen to be realized.   To go hence to
Cuba is not merely passing over a few degrees of latitude in
a few days' sail,— it is a step from the nineteenth century
back into the dark ages.   In the clime of sun and endless
summer, we are in the land of starless political darkness.
Lying under the lee of a land where every man is a sovereign, is a realm where the lives, liberties, and fortunes of
all are held at the tenure of the will of a single individual,
and whence not a single murmur of complaint can reach the
ear of the nominal ruler more than a thousand leagues away
in another hemisphere.   In close proximity to a country
where the taxes, self-imposed, are so light as to be almost
unfelt, is one where each free family pays nearly four hundred dollars per annum for the support of a system of bigoted tyranny, yielding in the aggregate an annual revenue
of twenty-five millions of dollars for which they receive no
equivalent, — no representation, no utterance, for pen and
tongue are alike proscribed,— no honor, no office, no emolument; while their industry is crippled, their intercourse

with other nations hampered in every way, their bread literally snatched from their lips, the freedom of education denied, and every generous, liberal aspiration of the human soul stifled in its birth. And this in the nineteenth century, and in North America.

Such are the contrasts, broad and striking, and such the reflections forced upon the mind of the citizen of the United States in Cuba. Do they never occur to the minds of the Creoles? We are told that they are willing slaves. Spain tells us so, and she extols to the world with complacent mendacity the loyalty of her " *siempre fielissima isla de Cuba.*" But why does she have a soldier under arms for every four white adults? We were about to say, white male citizens, but there are no citizens in Cuba. A proportionate military force in this country would give us a standing army of more than a million bayonets, with an annual expenditure, reckoning each soldier to cost only two hundred dollars per annum, of more than two hundred millions of dollars. And this is the peace establishment of Spain in Cuba — for England and France and the United States are all her allies, and she has no longer to fear the roving buccaneers of the Gulf who once made her tremble in her island fastness. For whom then is this enormous warlike preparation? Certainly for no external enemy,— there is none. The question answers itself,— it is for her very loyal subjects, the people of Cuba, that the queen of Spain makes all this warlike show.

19

It is impossible to conceive of any degree of loyalty that would be proof against the unparalleled burthens and atrocious system by which the mother country has ever loaded and weighed down her western colonists. They must be either more or less than men if they still cherish attachment to a foreign throne under such circumstances. But the fact simply is, the Creoles of Cuba are neither angels nor brutes; they are, it is true, a long-suffering and somewhat indolent people, lacking in a great degree the stern qualities of the Anglo-Saxon and the Anglo-Norman races, but nevertheless intelligent, if wanting culture, and not without those noble aspirations for independence and freedom, destitute of which they would cease to be men, justly forfeiting all claim to our sympathy and consideration. During the brief intervals in which a liberal spirit was manifested towards the colony by the home government, the Cubans gave proof of talent and energy, which, had they been permitted to attain their full development, would have given them a highly honorable name and distinguished character. When the field for genius was comparatively clear, Cuba produced more than one statesman and man of science, who would have done honor to a more favored land.

But these cheering rays of light were soon extinguished, and the fluctuating policy of Spain settled down into the rayless and brutal despotism which has become its normal condition, and a double darkness closed upon the political and intellectual prospects of Cuba. But the people are not,

and have not been the supine and idle victims of tyranny
which Spain depicts them.   The reader, who has indul-
gently followed us thus far, will remember the several times
they have attempted, manacled as they are, to free their
limbs from the chains that bind them.   It is insulting and
idle to say that they might have been free if they had earnestly desired and made the effort for freedom.   Who can say
what would have been the result of our own struggle for
independence, if Great Britain, at the outset, had been as
well prepared for resistance as Spain has always been in
Cuba? Who can say how long and painful would have
been the struggle, if one of the most powerful military
nations of Europe had not listened to our despairing appeal,
and thrown the weight of her gold and her arms into the
scale against our great enemy? When we see how — as
we do clearly — in a single night the well-contrived schemes
of an adroit and unprincipled knave enslaved a brilliant and
war-like people, like the French, who had more than once
tasted the fruits of republican glory and liberty, who had
borne their free flag in triumph over more than half of
Europe, we can understand why the Cubans, overawed from
the very outset, by the presence of a force vastly greater in
proportion than that which enslaved France, have been
unable to achieve their deliverance.   Nay, more — when we ·
consider the system pursued by the government of the
island, the impossibility of forming assemblages, and of con-
certing action, the presence of troops and spies everywhere,

the compulsory silence of the press — the violation of the sanctity of correspondence, the presence of a slave population, we can only wonder that any effort has been made, any step taken in that fatal pathway of revolution which leads infallibly to the *garrote*.

If Cuba lies at present under the armed heel of despotism we may be sure that the anguish of her sons is keenly aggravated by their perfect understanding of our own liberal institutions, and an earnest, if fruitless desire to participate in their enjoyment. It is beyond the power of the Spanish government to keep the people of the island in a state of complete darkness, as it seems to desire to do. The young men of Cuba educated at our colleges and schools, the visitors from the United States, and American merchants established on the island, are all so many apostles of republicanism, and propagandists of treason and rebellion. Nor can the captains-general with all their vigilance, exclude what they are pleased to call incendiary newspapers and documents from pretty extensive circulation among the " ever faithful." That liberal ideas and hatred of Spanish despotism are widely entertained among the Cubans is a fact no one who has passed a brief period among them can truthfully deny. The writer of these pages avers, from his personal knowledge, that they await only the means and the opportunity to rise in rebellion against Spain. We are too far distant to see more than the light smoke, but those who have trodden the soil of Cuba have sounded the depths of the volcano. The history of the unfortunate Lopez expedition proves nothing contrary to this. The force under Lopez afforded too weak a nucleus, was too hastily thrown upon the island, too ill prepared, and too untimely attacked, to enable the native patriots to rally round its standard, and thus to second the efforts of the invaders. With no ammunition nor arms to spare, recruits would have only added to the embarrassment of the adventurers. Yet had Lopez been joined by the brave but unfortunate Crittenden, with what arms and ammunition he possessed, had he gained some fastness where he could have been disciplining his command, until further aid arrived, the adventure might have had a very different termination from what we have recorded in an early chapter of this book.

Disastrous as was the result of the Lopez expedition, it nevertheless proved two important facts : first, the bravery of the Cubans, a small company of whom drove the enemy at the point of the bayonet; and, secondly, the inefficiency of Spanish troops when opposed by resolute men. If a large force of picked Spanish troops were decimated and routed in two actions, by a handful of ill-armed and undisciplined men, taken by surprise, we are justified in believing that if an effective force of ten thousand men, comprising the several arms, of cavalry, artillery, and infantry, had been thrown into the island, they would have carried all before them. With such a body of men to rally upon, the Cubans would have risen in the departments of the island, and her best transatlantic jewel would have been torn from the diadem of Spain.

That the Spanish government lives in constant dread of a renewal of the efforts on the part of Americans and exiled Cubans to aid the disaffected people of the island in throwing off its odious yoke, is a notorious fact, and there are evidences in the conduct of its officials towards those of this government that it regards the latter as secretly favoring such illegal action. Yet the steps taken by our government to crush any such attempts have been decided enough to satisfy any but a jealous and unreasonable power. President Fillmore, in his memorable proclamation, said, " Such expeditions can only be regarded as adventures for plunder and robbery," and declaring Americans who engaged in them outlaws, informed them that " they would forfeit their claim to the protection of this government, or any interference in their behalf, no matter to what extremity they might be reduced in consequence of their illegal conduct." In accordance with this declaration, the brave Crittenden and his men were allowed to be shot at Atares, though they were not taken with arms in their hands, had abandoned the expedition, and were seeking to escape from the island.

In a similar spirit the present chief magistrate alluded to our relations with Spain in his inaugural address, in the following explicit terms : —

" Indeed it is not to be disguised that our attitude as a nation, and our position on the globe, render the acquisition of certain possessions, not within our jurisdiction, eminently important, if not, in the future, essential for the preservation of the rights of commerce and the peace of the world. Should they be obtained, it will be through no grasping spirit, but with a view to obvious national interest and security, and in a manner entirely consistent with the strictest observance of national faith."

A recent proclamation, emanating from the same source, and warning our citizens of the consequences of engaging in an invasion of the island, also attests the determination to maintain the integrity of our relations with an allied power.

No candid student of the history of our relations with Spain can fail to be impressed by the frank and honorable attitude of our government, or to contrast its acts with those of the Spanish officials of Cuba. A history of the commercial intercourse of our citizens with the island would be a history of petty and also serious annoyances and grievances to which they have been subjected for a series of years by the Spanish officials, increasing in magnitude as the latter have witnessed the forbearance and magnanimity of our government. Not an American merchant or captain, who has had dealings with Cuba, but could furnish his list of insults and outrages, some in the shape of illegal extortions and delays, others merely gratuitous ebullitions of spite and malice dictated by a hatred of our country and its citizens. Of late instances of outrage so flagrant have occurred, that the executive has felt bound to call the attention of Congress to them in a message, in which he points out the great evil which lies at the bottom, and also the remedy.

" The offending party," he says, " is at our doors with large power for aggression, but none, it is alleged, for reparation.   The source of redress is in another hemisphere ; and the answers to our just complaints, made to the home government, are but the repetition of excuses rendered by inferior officials to the superiors, in reply to the representations of misconduct.   In giving extraordinary power to them, she owes it to justice, and to her friendly relations to this government, to guard with great vigilance against the exorbitant exercise of these powers, and in case of injuries to provide for prompt redress."

It is very clear that if, in such cases as the seizure of a vessel and her cargo by the port officers at Havana, for an alleged violation of revenue laws, or even port usages, redress, in case of official misconduct, can only be had by reference to the home government in another part of the world, our trade with Cuba will be completely paralyzed. The delay and difficulty in obtaining such redress has already, in too many cases, prompted extortion on the one hand, and acquiescence to injustice on the other.   The experience of the last four years alone will fully sustain the truth of this assertion.

In 1851 two American vessels were seized off Yucatan by the Spanish authorities on suspicion of being engaged in the Lopez expedition; in the same year the steamship Falcon was wantonly fired upon by a Spanish government vessel; in 1852 the American mail bags were forcibly opened and their contents examined by order of the captain-general; and less than two years ago, as is well known, the Crescent City was not allowed to land her passengers and mails, simply because the purser, Smith, was obnoxious to the government of the island. The Black Warrior, fired into on one voyage, was seized lately for a violation of a custom house form — an affair not yet, it is believed, settled with the Spanish government. More than once, on specious pretexts, have American sailors been taken from American vessels and thrown into Spanish prisons. In short, the insults offered by Spanish officials to our flag have so multiplied of late that the popular indignation in the country has reached an alarming height.

It is difficult for a republic and a despotism, situated like the United States and Cuba, to live on neighborly terms; and to control the indignation of the citizens of the former, proud and high spirited, conscious of giving no offence, and yet subjected to repeated insults, is a task almost too great for the most adroit and pacific administration. When we add to this feeling among our people a consciousness that Cuba, the source of all this trouble, is in unwilling vassalage to Spain, and longing for annexation to the United States, that under our flag the prosperity of her people would be secured, a vast addition made to our commercial resources,

an invaluable safeguard given to our southern frontier, and
the key to the Mississippi and the great west made secure
forever, we can no longer wonder at the spread of the conviction that Cuba should belong to this country, and this
too as soon as can be honorably brought about.   Had she
possessed more foresight and less pride, Spain would have
long since sold the island to the United States, and thereby
have relieved herself of a weighty care and a most dangerous property.

"So far from being really injured by the loss of the isl-
and," says Hon. Edward Everett, in his able and well
known letter to the British minister rejecting the proposition for the tripartite convention, "there is no doubt that,
were it peacefully transferred to the United States, a pros-
perous commerce between Cuba and Spain, resulting from
ancient associations and common language and tastes, would
be far more productive than the best contrived system of
colonial taxation.   Such, notoriously, has been the result to
Great Britain of the establishment of the independence of
the United States."

If it be true that the American minister at Madrid has
been authorized to offer a price nothing short of a royal
ransom for the island, we cannot conceive that the greedy
queen, and even the Cortes of Spain, would reject it, unless
secretly influenced by the powers which had the effrontery to
propose for our acceptance the tripartite treaty, by which we
were expected to renounce forever all pretension to the posses-

sion of Cuba. It is difficult to believe that France and England could for a moment seriously suppose that such a ridiculous proposition would be for one moment entertained by this government, and yet they must so have deceived themselves, or otherwise they would not have made the proposition as they did.

Of the importance, not to say necessity, of the possession of Cuba by the United States, statesmen of all parties are agreed; and they are by no means in advance of the popular sentiment; indeed, the class who urge its immediate acquisition, at any cost, by any means, not as a source of wealth, but as a political necessity, is by no means inconsiderable. It would be foreign to our purpose to quote the opinions of any ultraists, nor do we design, in these closing remarks, to enter the field of politics, or political discussion. We have endeavored to state facts only, and to state them plainly, deducing the most incontrovertible conclusions.

We find the following remarks in a recent conservative speech of Mr. Latham, a member of Congress, from California. They present, with emphasis, some of the points we have lightly touched upon:

" I admit that our relations with Spain, growing out of that island (Cuba), are of an extremely delicate nature; that the fate of that island, its misgovernment, its proximity to our shores, and the particular institutions established upon it, are of vast importance to the peace and security of this country; and that the utmost vigilance in regard to it is not only demanded by prudence, but an act of imperative duty on the part of our government. The island of Cuba commands, in a measure, the Gulf of Mexico. In case of a maritime war, in which the United States may be engaged, its possession by the enemy might become a source of infinite annoyance to us, crippling our shipping, threatening the great emporium of our southern commerce, and exposing our whole southern coast, from the capes of Florida to the mouth of the Rio Grande, to the enemy's cruisers. The geographical position of Cuba is such that we cannot, without a total disregard to our own safety, permit it to pass into the hands of any first-class power; nay, that it would be extremely imprudent to allow it to pass even into the hands of a power of the second rank, possessed of energy and capacity for expansion."

If Cuba come into our possession peaceably, as the fruits of a fair bargain, or as a free-will offering of her sons, after a successful revolution, we can predict for her a future as bright as her past has been desolate and gloomy; for the union of a territory with a foreign population to our confederacy is no new and doubtful experiment. Louisiana, with her French and Spanish Creoles, is one of the most reliable states of the Union; and, not long after her admission, she signed, with her best blood, the pledge of fealty to the common country.

More recently, we all remember how, when Taylor, in the presence of the foe upon the Rio Grande, called for volunteers, the gallant Creoles rushed to arms, and crowded to his banner. The Creoles of Cuba are of the same blood and lineage,— Spaniards in chivalry of soul, without the ferocity and fanaticism of the descendants of the Cid. We are sure, from what they have shown in the past, that liberal institutions will develop latent qualities which need only free air for their expansion. They will not want companions, friends and helpers. A tide of emigration from the States will pour into the island, the waste lands will be reclaimed, and their hidden wealth disclosed; a new system of agricultural economy will be introduced; the woods of the island will furnish material for splendid ships; towns and villages will rise with magical celerity, and the whole surface of the " garden of the world " will blossom like the rose.

" Rich in soil, salubrious in climate, varied in productions, the home of commerce," says the Hon. O. R. Singleton, of Mississippi, " Cuba seems to have been formed to become ' the very button on Fortune's cap.' Washed by the Gulf-stream on half her borders, with the Mississippi pouring out its rich treasures on one side, and the Amazon, destined to become a ' cornucopia,' on the other,— with the ports of Havana and Matanzas on the north, and the Isle of Pines and St. Jago de Cuba on the south, Nature has written upon her, in legible characters, a destiny far above that of a subjugated province of a rotten European dynasty. Her home is in the bosom of the North American confed-

eracy.   Like a lost Pleiad, she may wander on for a few
months or years in lawless, chaotic confusion; but, ulti-
mately, the laws of nature and of nations will vindicate
themselves, and she will assume her true social and political condition, despite the diplomacy of statesmen, the trick-
ery of knaves, or the frowns of tyrants.   Cuba will be free.
The spirit is abroad among her people; and, although they
dare not give utterance to their thoughts, lest some treacherous breeze should bear them to a tyrant's ears, still they
think and feel, and will act when the proper time shall
arrive.   The few who have dared 'to do or die' have fallen,
and their blood still marks the spot where they fell.   Such
has been the case in all great revolutionary struggles.
Those who lead the van must expect a sharp encounter
before they break through the serried hosts of tyranny, and
many a good man falls upon the threshold of the temple.

> " ' But freedom's battle once begun,
> Bequeathed from bleeding sire to son,
> Though baffled oft, is always won.' "